Human–Computer Interaction Series

SpringerBriefs in Human-Computer Interaction

Editors-in-Chief

Desney Tan
Microsoft Research, Redmond, WA, USA

Jean Vanderdonckt
Louvain School of Management, Université catholique de Louvain,
Louvain-La-Neuve, Belgium

More information about this subseries at http://www.springer.com/series/15580

Guy André Boy

Design for Flexibility

A Human Systems Integration Approach

Guy André Boy
CentraleSupélec
Paris-Saclay University
Gif-sur-Yvette, France

ESTIA Institute of Technology
Bidart, France

ISSN 1571-5035   ISSN 2524-4477 (electronic)
Human–Computer Interaction Series
ISSN 2520-1670   ISSN 2520-1689 (electronic)
SpringerBriefs in Human-Computer Interaction
ISBN 978-3-030-76390-9   ISBN 978-3-030-76391-6 (eBook)
https://doi.org/10.1007/978-3-030-76391-6

This Springer imprint is published by the registered company Springer Nature Switzerland AG
The registered company address is: Gewerbestrasse 11, 6330 Cham, Switzerland

Preface

The content of this book is strongly influenced by a compilation of presentations I have made over the past two decades, current results of the INCOSE[1] Human–System Integration Working Group, which I have the privilege of coordinating, and my current work within the FlexTech Program I lead at CentraleSupélec and ESTIA Institute of Technology. This work addresses the issue of flexibility in our current and future digital societies from the perspective of human systems integration (HSI).

Our increasing need for flexibility has emerged from the uses of new digital technologies, which are constantly expanding, and from the need to maintain the values of freedom and ethics. It should be noted that while these new digital technologies are of great service to us, they also introduce constraints, rigidity and a possible disconnection with reality. There is a risk of losing a certain "common sense."

"Common sense is nothing more than a deposit of prejudices laid down in the mind before age eighteen!" I have often thought of this statement by Albert Einstein,[2] remembering what some shepherds of the Pyrenees used to say to me when we were caring for the sheep on the mountainsides. They taught me proverbs to predict the weather the next day, such as, for example: "Red sky at night, shepherds delight," which means that when the sky becomes red at night, the weather will be good the day after.

I tried to apply these maxims myself, but very often to no avail. I would come back to the shepherds and tell them about my misadventures. They laughed with all their heart, saying: "But you haven't looked at the sky properly, my friend!" In the evening, they showed me the sky, explaining that if it was red, but this time the sun was reflecting on the clouds, then a different proverb had to be used: "The sun looks at itself, beware of the rain!" All this in Occitan of course! I was less than 18 years old! I actually found these shepherds full of "common sense" when the use of these heuristics worked.

---

[1] International Council on Systems Engineering (https://www.incose.org/).

[2] Barnett, L. (1948). The Universe and Dr. Einstein: Part II. *Harper's Magazine*, Volume 196 (microfilm). Harper & Brothers Publishers, New York. (retrieved 26-05-2020: https://quoteinvestigator.com/2014/04/29/common-sense).

Is this the "common sense" that my friends, the shepherds of the Pyrenees, taught me before I was 18 years old and which I still have today when I use my critical mind to make sense of calculations or experimental results of my research work? What really appeals to me is this combination of experiences, often accumulated and passed down through generations in the form of heuristics and rigorous rationalizations, often based on mathematics and logic, which seem to me to be deeply necessary to ensure results that "make sense." Meaning is more in the qualitative than in the quantitative, and every time we make "scholarly" calculations, we must always interpret them (i.e., give them meaning and therefore a good dose of subjectivity). This subjectivity is made up of profound experience acquired and compiled over time. I always found this kind of knowledge and knowhow, when constantly tested and carefully compiled, provides extensive flexibility in everyday activities. Of course, such tests and compilation are always very context-dependent (i.e., knowledge and associated knowhow are tested and compiled in specific contexts, which can or cannot be incrementally generalized)—this is one of the limitations of educated common sense.

It took me many years of studies and research to, one day, come across a book presenting the Arts of Memory of the ancient Greeks, the book by Frances Yates (Yates 2014, originally published in 1966). The ancient Greeks transmitted knowledge using mnemonic processes[3] that combined observable real objects with abstractions. This practice of transmitting knowledge continued practically until the 20th century, during which René Descartes' Discourse on Method, enunciated in 1610, gradually erased this part of ancestral practices. What is remarkable today is that the Internet, an external associative memory, but also a pure technological invention product of Descartes' Discourse of the Method, brings us back to the Arts of Memory through its use, because we need to associate "bookmarks," icons and other "reminders," to guide us in our searches on the Web, and thus associate concrete objects with abstractions. But how do we develop "common sense" in this context?

At this point, I'd like to share my NASA experience with you. I have had the good fortune and honor of working with some of the players in the Apollo program, long after their exploits of course. I learned humility. Beyond the extraordinary financial investment, why has a program like Apollo been such a global success? The first answer is preparation, flexibility and great commitment of the people involved.

It took about four days to fly to the moon. Twelve human beings walked on the moon between July 1969 and December 1972. Apollo teams were mainly made up of young pilots, engineers and scientists with experience in civil and/or military aviation who absorbed the training like sponges. Anytime I had the chance to discuss with some of them, I saw an extreme commitment, empathy and competence. The ground crew was always seen as an extension of the spacecraft crew; they had a deep respect for the flight crew and vice versa. The greatest strength of these men was their constant situational awareness and fear of making mistakes. Teamwork was

---

[3] A mnemonic process is a way to remember something using, for example, the method of loci of using a familiar physical location like a house and putting things to remember in locations of the house.

based on trust, discipline, and the slogan: "You must fly as you train,"[4] which meant a lot of hard work ahead. Debriefings were open, honest and complete. Feedback and corrective action for future flights were prompt (Griffin 2010).

An essential concept in the implementation of large projects and risky programs is trust between the human beings involved but also trust in the technologies used and the organizational set up. Without trust, there can be no effective collaboration, at least not in a free and accepted way. Overcoming failures requires resilience, and this is a quality required to bring any ambitious project to a successful conclusion. Needless to say, the Apollo 1 mission was a disaster in which the three astronauts perished in their burning capsule on launch pad 39 at Cape Canaveral, Florida, and there were 16 flights that followed, including Apollo 11, which, for the first time in human history, allowed two men, Neil Armstrong and Buzz Aldrin, to walk on the Moon in July 1969.

Where do we stand on this "common sense" made of accumulated, articulated, implemented and tested experiences? Going to the moon was a unique experience. In the beginning, of course, there was no common sense based on experience, because there was no experience at all in this field. They had to think, build concepts on assumptions and then act. The logical mechanism of abduction was in the forefront. Calculations, models and simulations were needed to build all the equipment necessary for the missions. Also, the setting up of flight management processes and the development of survival protocols, often carried out in real time in the event of abnormal situations, as was the case for Apollo 13. This "common sense" was built dynamically, in an agile manner, by chance and necessity, as Jacques Monod would have said, but also by the collaboration of competent and motivated teams.

How do we keep this "experience-based common sense" alive, changeable and evolving? Since Apollo, very few programs of this kind have been developed. On the contrary, we have experienced increasingly short-term projects, forcing the actors to be reactive to current situations based on short-term financial objectives, rather than being proactive based on humanistic goals.

Before the COVID-19 pandemic, we were still focused on a large automation replacement of humans by "autonomous" machines, such as autonomous vehicles. Today, we are thinking about rebuilding a world more oriented towards a balance between nature and more sustainable technology. This awareness is more tangible than ever. Are we going to design and develop aircraft that are more environmentally friendly? I think we have no choice, and aeronautics is not the only industrial sector affected by this issue. Future developments in sustainable technology will have to satisfy strong environmental, social and economic constraints.

It should be noted that although aeronautics was born and developed thanks to air and space enthusiasts, the last two decades have seen the financial management of aeronautical companies rise to the point of favoring sales at the expense of research. I hope COVID-19 crisis will contribute to change that. We're going to have to build greener aircraft, bringing the human and societal aspects to the forefront, and of

---

[4] You must do your task in earnest in the same way that you train to do it. This is what Jerry Griffin, a former NASA Flight Director, told us that they did all the time in the Apollo program.

course, balancing the economic side of things. We're going to have to move from techno-centric engineering to human-centered design. We're going to have to rethink the question of mobility in truly ecological and societal terms.

The FlexTech program is now in the running to participate in defining the founding principles of Human System Integration (HSI) in this new paradigm. HSI is indispensable in the century ahead, starting with societal technological integration. Let's stop making technology for engineers! Let's stop making money for money as the financial managers and shareholders of large commercial institutions continue to dictate! We will have to innovate. Despite all the precautions and anticipations, there always comes a time when we have to decide and take a risk in order to act; preparation is essential in taking a risk (Boy and Brachet 2010). The FlexTech program approach is centered on common sense based on experience, "a good sense of experience," which is itself based on preparation, trust and collaboration. This book proposes clues, concepts and approaches to make our sociotechnical systems more flexible and further develop this new sustainable paradigm.

There are many reasons to acknowledge and thank the people who helped in making this book a reality. This book is a primer for the first rationalization of the content of FlexTech program that includes a research and education program, as well as the ESTIA Concept Lab (CLE). The first people's names that come to my mind are Cynthia Lamothe, Helen Huard de la Marre, Patxi Elissalde, Bernard Yannou. Olivier Gicquel, Philippe Dufourq, and Jean-Patrick Gaviard. Thanks to Dassault Systèmes Foundation for their support in the initial setup of CLE.

Many people supported me directly or indirectly on the topic of this book during this last year, but also during the years before, and I would like to recognize them. Among them are Adam Abdin, Audrey Abi Akle, David Atkinson, Thierry Baron, Anne Barros, Eric Bartoli, Thierry Bellet, Michael Boardman, Sébastien Boulnois, Jeremy Boy, Perrine Boy, Divya Madhavan Brochier, Stélian Camara Dit Pinto, Nadine Couture, Françoise Darses, Ken Davidian, Bernardo Delicado, Bruno Depardon, Julien Dezemery, Jaime Diaz Pineda, Francis Durso, Mica Endsley, Alain Garcia, Jean-Patrick Gaviard, Eapen George, Ami Harel, Avi Harel, Daniel Hauret, Andreas Makoto Hein, Marija Jancovic, Grace Kennedy, Daniel Krob, Bertrand Lantes, Olivier Larre, Benoît Le Blanc, Jérémy Legardeur, Larry Leifer, Ludovic Loine, Raymond Lu Cong Sang, Kerry Lunney, Dimitri Masson, Christophe Merlo, Peter Moertl, Kathleen Mosier, Jean-Michel Munoz, Marc Musen, Donald Norman, Philippe Palanque, David Pappalardo, Jean Pinet, Edwige Quillerou-Grivot, Jérôme Ranc, Garry Roedler, Jean-Claude Roussel, Alexander Rudolph, Anabela Simoes, François Thermy, Laetitia Urfels, Eric Villeneuve, Terry Winograd, and Avigdor Zonnenshain. I also would like to thank anonymous reviewers who helped improving the quality of this book.

Finally, thank you, Marie-Catherine for your patience and love, you helped me making this book a reality through endless discussions.

Paris, France   Guy André Boy
March 2021

References

Boy GA, Brachet G (2010) Risk taking: a human necessity that needs to be managed. Dossier. Air
    and Space Academy, France
Griffin G (2010) Crew-Ground Integration in Piloted Space Programs. Keynote at HCI-Aero'10,
    Cape Canaveral, Florida, USA
Yates F (2014) The Art of Memory. Random House, U.K. ISBN-13: 978-1847922922

Contents

Acronyms

AAAI	Association for the Advancement of Artificial Intelligence
ADD	Active Design Documents
AI	Artificial Intelligence
AI4SE	Artificial Intelligence for Systems Engineering
AUTOS	Artifact, User, Task, Organization, Situation (pyramid model)
BPMN	Business Process Model Notation
CFA	Cognitive Function Analysis
CPSFA	Cognitive Physical Structure Function Analysis
CSCW	Computer Supported Cooperative Work
DC	Design Card
DTM	Design team Member
FMS	Flight Management System
FTP	File Transfer Protocol
GEM	Group Elicitation Method
GP	General Practitioner
GPS	Global Positioning System
HCD	Human-Centered Design
HCI	Human-Computer Interaction
HFE	Human Factors and Ergonomics
HITLS	Human-In-The-Loop Simulation
HSI	Human Systems Integration
HTTP	HyperText Transfer Protocol
IHU	Institut Hospitalo Universitaire (University Hospital Institute)
KBS	Knowledge-Based Systems
M2020	Mars 2020 rover, now called Perseverance
MAS	Multi Agent System
MBSE	Model Based Systems Engineering
NAIR	Natural-Artificial Intentional-Reactive Framework
ND	Navigation Display
PCR	Polymerase Chain Reaction
SE	Systems Engineering
SE4AI	Systems Engineering for Artificial Intelligence

SEIR	*Susceptible → Exposed → Infected → Recovered (model)*
SFAC	Structure-Function Abstract-Concrete Framework
SIM	Systemic Interaction Models
SimBSE	Simulation Based Systems Engineering
SoS	System of Systems
TOP	Technology, Organization and People (model)
UML	Unified Modeling Language

List of Figures

Chapter 1
Introduction

Abstract In my 2013 book, *Orchestrating Human-Centered Design*, I was already advocating the need to take into account complexity science and problem-solving techniques to streamline unusual situations where commonly accepted procedures no longer work. This book expands most concepts and methods based on cognitive engineering to a new set based on current developments of human systems integration (HSI). Furthermore, based on experience, *"experience-based common sense"* (i.e., what I also called *educated common sense*), must prevail and is appropriately combined with real-world data. This approach is called abduction (Peirce in Collected papers of Charles Sanders Peirce (1931–1958) In: Hartshorne C, Weiss P, Burks A (eds) Harvard University Press, Cambridge, MA), a logical inference mechanism that requires us to anticipate possible futures, choose one, and demonstrate that we can reach it using the means available as well as other ones we develop.

1.1 Dealing with the Unexpected

Although I worked on the ideas, concepts and approaches developed in this book long before we experienced the COVID-19 pandemic, the starkness of this pandemic makes it an ideal point of focus. Indeed, this pandemic has challenged most traditional ways of crisis management.[1]

COVID-19 taught us one more time that the metaphor of the Black Swan (Taleb 2007) is useful for understanding an unforeseen, exceptional and/or extreme situation when we are not prepared to deal with it. How do we prepare for it? In this book, I will not try to provide short-term procedures, but longer-term models and tools that could support our understanding of the co-evolution of people, technology, environment,

---

[1] That is, perceiving what we can pick up with our senses, searching for what we do not understand, making sense of what we can gradually rationalize and finally understand, projecting ourselves into possible futures and those of our environment, modeling them, simulating them, trying to define trajectories that will enable us to reach them, and so on, based on strong experience-based models.

society and economy.[2] Most often, we will consider technology and economy as the main variables to be considered and optimized, leaving aside people, environment and society (e.g., people's well-being, safety and comfort; the diversity and biological stability of the environment; harmony and trust within society). Today, most countries optimize the lives of their citizens in terms of technology and economy, considering people, environment and society as adjustment variables[3] or constraints, when the reverse should be the case.

COVID-19 revealed how fragile a country is when procedures are rigid and cannot be easily changed. The health of individuals should not be used as an adjustment variable. In this crisis situation, people's health suddenly became a dependent variable to be optimized. This radical change is not easy to understand and correct when it occurs suddenly. Coping with the unexpected (Pinet 2015) has become a reality that needs to be better understood and managed in ultra-safe systems such as commercial aviation, compared to medicine for example (Amalberti et al. 2005). Conventional engineering methods dictated by financial requirements will not succeed in this endeavor. This homeostatic system inevitably leads to a break with freedom towards a rigid order, which is often maintained by repression. Instead, we need people's trust, collaboration and motivation to solve unexpected problems together. In short, we need flexibility in technology, organization and people. Sociotechnical flexibility does not happen by chance; it must be prepared, built and maintained.

COVID-19 has taught us humility and realism to face a pandemic that has blocked the economies of many countries at the same time and around the world. These things can happen! Wow! Nature comes back to tell us that we do not master everything through our economy and our technologies. They are far too rigid to adapt to a sudden, non-linear problem. Nature is an open, non-linear, self-organizing system. On the contrary, our economy and technologies are based on reductionist, quasi-closed and rigid processes. We have realized that complexity cannot be reduced to mathematical formulae, even non-linear ones, because they cannot encompass the interconnectedness of all possible relevant parameters in space and time. We are far from being able to understand the emergence of unexpected behaviors, properties and functions. Consequently, we still have a lot of work to do in the field of complexity theories.

COVID-19, therefore, highlighted the urgent need to teach complexity in school instead of focusing almost exclusively on linear algebra! Complexity is about interdependent systems that behave like living organisms. We urgently need to be able to describe complex systems in terms of compatible naturalistic and artificial concepts. To use the metaphor of the orchestra where life is music, we need to invent a music theory (Boy 2013). We also need to allot musicians, conductors, composers, scores,

[2]Abductive reasoning is a logical inference that seeks to find the simplest and most likely conclusion from the observations based on heuristics coming from experience. In cognitive psychology, abduction is a form of intuitive reasoning that consists in suppressing improbable solutions. This notion is opposed to a logic of systematic search exploration.

[3]An adjustment variable is a resource used by an economic agent to reduce a temporary imbalance between the means at its disposal and the commitments it has entered into.

audience, etc. We need to observe the real world and elicit its regularities and inconsistencies to better develop knowledge models that will enable realistic simulations that recreate and reflect what we have observed. This is difficult and labor-intensive, but it is mandatory if we want to live in our increasingly complex world, where nature and artifacts are becoming more and more closely associated. The term "artifact" is used in this book to refer to any entity designed and manufactured by people (i.e., an artificial system). An artifact can be physical and/or cognitive (i.e., conceptual). Some artifacts can be very useful and beneficial to nature and humans; others can be dangerous to our planet Earth and our species.

COVID-19 taught us responsibility. What kind of technology should we design and develop to ensure greater safety, efficiency and comfort? Could a COVID-19 type pandemic be prevented or better managed in the future? How can we learn more about the causes in order to better manage them? Why is this pandemic problem a serious twenty-first century issue (Fauci 2001)? What are the right adjustment variables for humanity? Who is responsible? How should we approach these questions and answer them correctly? How can we replace our unbridled race to short-term technological development with a sociotechnical approach that is both humanistic and ecological in the long term? Considering that our cortex gives us the capacity to create and explore, how far should we go in terms of innovation? What types of artifacts should we develop for the good of humanity and planet Earth?

1.2 Flexibility in Human Systems Integration

Although fortuitous, the coincidence of questions related to COVID-19 and the themes of this book enabled me to introduce this new discipline that is human systems integration (HSI) in a more tangible manner, in the sense that the management of the unexpected (Boy 2013) opens the field of risk taking seen from the angle of abduction (Boy and Brachet 2010). We will therefore deal with HSI in its broadest sense. HSI is at the crossroads of several disciplines, including psychology, social sciences, biology, mathematics, computer science and the engineering sciences. Models from these initial disciplines are already and will be selected and modified to form more integrated theories. The resulting basic framework will be used to propose solutions to improve the flexibility of our sociotechnical systems (e.g., medical systems, mobility systems, education systems, police, defense and many others).

A lot of work has been done on automation and its drawbacks (Bainbridge 1987; Sarter et al. 1997). This book introduces the mandatory shift from rigid automation to flexible autonomy, requiring a new HSI approach. The rationalization of this shift was born from the analysis of accidents and the management of the unexpected. It is very difficult to write a book, which will be read in a linear way, where content is highly non-linear, as reflected in Fig. 1.1, which provides the links between many concepts, frameworks, models, and approaches necessary in design for flexibility. In addition, the sequential story presented in this book will be illustrated using examples from real-world studies that I have been involved in.

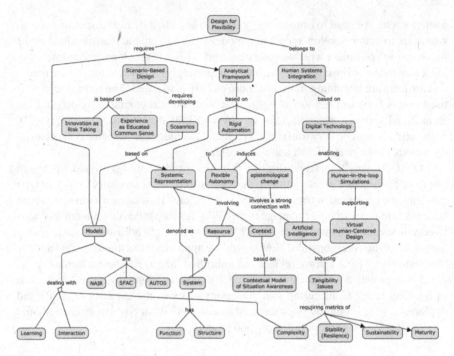

Fig. 1.1 A "design for flexibility" concept map

The concept of flexibility is important during the whole life cycle of the system (i.e., from early design to dismantling). The content of this book is interdisciplinary, based on engineering design, systems engineering, human factors and ergonomics, human–computer interaction, artificial intelligence, economics, ecology and philosophy.

Chapter 2 provides the approach that guides Virtual Human-Centered Design (VHCD) and a framework for flexibility analysis. One of the main roles of HSI is analysis, design and evaluation of complex human–machine systems with increasing autonomy. Chapter 3 provides an articulation of HSI, which requires mastering models (Chapter 4) and methodological clarifications (Chapter 5). The shift from rigid automation to flexible autonomy is motivated by the current evolution of digital technologies towards the control of cyber-physical systems tangibility, taking the Tangible Interactive Systems approach (Boy 2016). Chapter 6 develops the unavoidable issue of tangibility in contemporary systems engineering. Chapter 7 provides a synthesis of the book by presenting the need for a scenario-based approach to managing risks in the development and operations of complex sociotechnical systems. Concluding challenges will be provided on design for flexibility.

Design for flexibility is an important part of human systems integration, considered as an emerging discipline. The terminology used in this book comes from a cross-fertilization of several fields that deal with technology, organizations and people. Therefore, do not hesitate to use the glossary at the end of the book to find out the meaning of some terms.

References

Amalberti R, Aroy Y, Barach P, Berwick DM (2005) Five system barriers to achieving ultra-safe health care. Ann Intern Med 142(9):756–764

Bainbridge L (1987) Ironies of automation. In: Rasmussen J, Duncan K, Leplat J (eds) New technology and human error. John Wiley & Sons Ltd., Chicester, pp 271–283

Boy GA (2013) Orchestrating human-centered design. Springer, UK

Boy GA (2016) Tangible interactive systems: grasping the real world with computers. Springer, UK. ISBN: 978-3-319-30270-6

Boy GA, Brachet G (2010) Risk taking: a human necessity that needs to be managed. Dossier. Air and Space Academy, France

Fauci AS (2001). Infectious diseases: considerations for the 21st century. Clin Infect Dis 32(5):675–685. https://doi.org/10.1086/319235

Peirce CS (1931–1958) Collected papers of Charles Sanders Peirce. In: Hartshorne C, Weiss P, Burks A (eds) Harvard University Press, Cambridge, MA

Pinet J (2015) Facing the unexpected in flight: human limitations and interaction with technology in the cockpit. CRC Press. ISBN-13: 978-1498718714

Sarter NB, Woods DD, Billings CE (1997) Automation surprises. John Wiley and Sons, Handbook of human factors and ergonomics

Taleb NN (2007) The black swan: the impact of the highly improbable. Random House, New York. ISBN: 978-1-4000-6351-2. Expanded 2nd edn in 2010, ISBN: 978-0812973815

Chapter 2
A Framework for Flexibility Analysis in Sociotechnical Systems

Abstract We have entered a digital society that offers us more freedom but also enslaves us to a new sociotechnical environment for which we have not yet assumed all shortcomings. The characteristics of digital technology are essentially a function of the sociotechnical maturity of technologies that support it and its integration. This chapter emphasizes sociotechnical maturity and promotes the shift from rigid automation to flexible autonomy, which cannot be studied and developed without considering systems as a representation that articulates concepts such as structures, functions, contexts and resources. This representation is embedded into the so-called "context-resource orthogonality" framework where resources require to be explicitly formalized as objects or subjects, and contexts deal with various kinds of situations embedded into a contextual model of situation awareness. These concepts are illustrated by an example of a community-based health system.

2.1 From Rigid Automation to Flexible Autonomy

Increased automation during the 1980s created a number of rigidities in our daily lives. For example, menu-driven telephone answering machines provide us with a number of cascading options to take us to a given service. This type of system was designed and developed by engineers in the form of rigid computer algorithms, which unfortunately did not take into account all contexts of use that inevitably arise in operations, one day or another. As a result, we are faced with a closed and rigid system that does not allow any adaptation. Most of the time, we may call a support service that might sometimes answer us, possibly with a delay, in legalese void of context or meaning. This rigid automation must today be replaced by more flexible support (i.e., adaptable to the context). Without a human-centered approach (i.e., one that takes into account most meaningful usages), we cannot achieve this.

We have entered a digital society that offers us more freedom but also enslaves us to a new sociotechnical system for which we have not yet assumed all shortcomings. The characteristics of digital technology are essentially a function of sociotechnical maturity of technologies that support it and their integration. What is sociotechnical maturity? An immature technology used by non-experts imposes rigidity, simply because it has not yet been influenced by sufficient experience feedback: technical feedback, where we will talk about technological maturity (type 1); feedback on uses, where we will talk about maturity of practices (type 2); and feedback on the evolution of society and culture, where we will talk about societal maturity (type 3). These three types of maturity must inevitably be taken into account if we want to move towards greater autonomy within a sociotechnical system and, in other words, if we want to have more flexibility and fluidity in daily practices.

How to achieve more autonomy? The answer to this question lies in the definition of what we mean by "autonomy." Autonomy is precisely linked to maturity. If we talk about a person's autonomy, we are also talking about his or her maturity in relation to his or her life in a given environment. The legislation of some countries determines the maturity of citizens at the age of 18 and considers them as autonomous from that age (i.e., the time they are no longer legally dependent on their parents). In practice, they may still be dependent on their parents for a longer time. Becoming independent requires a considerable amount of learning and practice. Without education and training, it is difficult for a person to become independent. The same is true for a system in general, whether technological and/or organizational.

However, we have not yet answered the question of autonomy because we have not addressed it from a multi-agent perspective. Indeed, the hypothesis we are going to make is essential: we cannot talk about autonomy without talking about the environment in which it operates. In other words, a so-called "autonomous" system operates in its environment, composed of other systems, following a number of coordination rules. We will talk about the System of Systems (SoS) when we talk about this environment. Moreover, the more systems of an SoS become autonomous, the more coordination rules they require to operate safely, efficiently and comfortably.

If we consider the operational experience we have in the management of complex systems, we can identify three main processes (Fig. 2.1): two rigid processes that include procedure following and automation supervision; and problem-solving that should naturally be a flexible process.

Procedure-following consists of "automating" users or human operators (i.e., they have no choice but to follow operations procedures in well-defined contexts). Monitoring and management of automated machines consist of supervising machines that follow computerized procedures (i.e., human operators must ensure that the machines they are in charge of remain within an acceptable range of safety and efficiency). Problem-solving is used when the first two processes fail. It is typically performed by human operators, who must have the knowledge and skills to properly state and solve problems. This is referred to as autonomy, rather than human and machine automation. Autonomy requires a multi-functional approach (i.e., multi-agent), involving several types of skills that must be thought either intrinsically (i.e., agent's rarely-used specific resources that the agent must have learned and possibly experienced) or extrinsically (i.e., collaborating with other agents who/that have the required skills). These three major processes of managing complex systems lead us to the same conclusion: we need to better understand and implement an allocation of functions to the different agents or systems that allow for more flexibility and fluidity in the

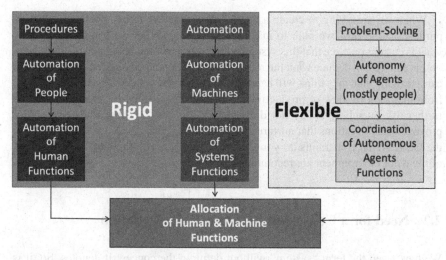

Fig. 2.1 Procedures, automation and problem-solving processes (Boy 2020)

control and management of resulting sociotechnical systems in normal, abnormal and emergency situations.

Procedure following and machine automation monitoring are rigid processes that make sense in well-defined contexts but lose their meaning outside these contexts. This is where the problem-solving process makes sense. The question is then to identify, develop and master the systems that will support this problem-solving process, which requires flexibility.

Solving a problem means stating it right. It is interesting to note that in school or university, we learn many methods for solving problems that are "well-stated in advance," without particularly learning how to state difficult problems. When we have learned all these problem-solving methods well, we have somehow automated or robotized ourselves to apply the procedures that constitute them. This means that the current situation must be stated in such a way that it "fits" well with the methods or procedures we have. In this approach to monitoring procedures, we may well be out of the loop if we do not know how to properly state unanticipated problems.

What does it mean to be a good problem solver? Stating a problem is above all being creative (i.e., making hypotheses and trying to verify them). We are most often confronted with trying to state a problem when the perceived situation is unexpected, unforeseen or unknown. In this case, we have to be creative. Creativity requires flexibility. What are the conceptual and technological tools available to us to ensure sufficient flexibility to create a solution? For example, imagine a painter facing her canvas. She has to create a new color, which she doesn't have on her palette. She needs an orange. She will mix, let's say integrate, red with yellow until she finds the orange hue that satisfies her. Creating is integrating! This integration is based on a set of tests and compensations until a performance criterion is met.

When we are trying to create a new system, we have to ask ourselves what its purpose is and how we plan to make it operational. What we can do is describe what is current practice that this system addresses, and what human errors have been observed. We can deduce what the requirements of human beings concerned are. We can ask them what they think will happen if the proposed system is ever implemented, from the point of view of productivity, aesthetics and safety, for example. We can further ask ourselves, "Why not do the work this way?" These are naïve and/or provocative suggestions that nurture critical thinking. We can also ask the experts in the field, "What constraints do you foresee?" In all cases, pragmatic investigations of the work environment are recommended.

2.2   Need for a Consistent Systemic Representation

We have used the term "system" without defining the concept it denotes. So, it is time to define it. We will call "system" a representation of any entity, natural or artificial, human or machine, individual or organizational. In terms of components and properties, a system (Fig. 2.2):

- accepts inputs, called (prescribed) tasks, and produces outputs, called (effective) activities;
- can be physical and/or cognitive;
- operates in an environment that is defined as a system of systems;
- has components that are themselves systems;
- is composed of a structure (which can be a structure of structures) and a function (which can be a function of functions).

We have become accustomed to confusing the notion of a system with that of a machine. In fact, a system can represent an entity that is natural and/or artificial. Medical doctors talk about the cardiovascular system or the neural system of a human being. Lawyers talk about the legal system of a country. Politicians talk about a

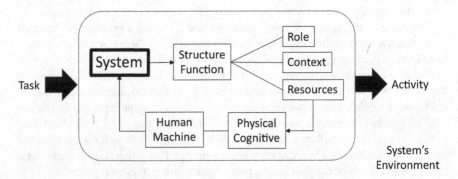

Fig. 2.2 Definition of a system in its environment

centralized or federal state system. It is sometimes difficult to extend the concept of a system to humans. However, in this book, we will consider a human being as a system composed of other systems, which may be natural (e.g., the human body includes organs, limbs and speech) or artificial (e.g., a pacemaker, a prosthesis). Symmetrically, a machine system may include human systems (e.g., an aircraft includes pilots and passengers).

Any function (idem structure) is defined by its role, its context of validity, and a set of resources. The resources of a function (or a structure) are systems. Therefore, a system is defined recursively as shown in Fig. 2.2:

$$\text{system} \rightarrow \text{structure/function} \rightarrow \text{resource} = \text{system}$$

The function of a system can be automatic or controlled, in the sense of Shiffrin and Schneider's seminal work on cognitive functions (Schneider and Shiffrin 1977; Shiffrin and Schneider 1977). We will say that an automatic function relies on a single resource that is procedurally preprogrammed, while a controlled function relies on a resource that includes a problem-solving algorithm, which in turn may rely on other internal or external resources.

We will say that a system is autonomous when it is supported by a set of necessary and sufficient resources to perform any task that leads to satisfactory activity in a given context. When this is not the case, it is necessary to use other systems to ensure that the initial task is carried out correctly. In this case, the system will not be said to be autonomous. However, it will become autonomous when it will integrate corresponding problem-solving capabilities and will not be obliged to request external help.

It is clear from this definition that it will be difficult, if not impossible, to build fully autonomous machine systems because it is impossible to implement a sufficient set of resources to ensure the production of the correct system's activity in all cases. For example, so-called "autonomous" vehicles will have to be thought of as controlled systems and not as fully automatic ones, except when they are operated in close, linear and fully organized (i.e., as opposed to open, non-linear and self-organized) environments (Taleb 2007; Klochko 2007).

A system has a structure and a function (Fig. 2.2). In previous writings, I have only defined the functional part of a system by its role, its context of validity and the associated resources (Boy 2013, 2020). The structural part of a system is defined in the same way. Indeed, any structure, or infrastructure, has a role (e.g., the structure of a house has the role of permanently separating its interior from its exterior), a context of validity (e.g., the structure of a house is defined for a life cycle of a certain number of years), and a set of resources (e.g., the structure of a house is made up of walls, floors, doors, and windows). In the same way, the cognitive structure of the human brain includes areas/resources for speech and others for vision, and so on.

At this level, two essential concepts emerge from the definition of a system: resources and contexts. These two concepts are orthogonal. I propose to name this association of concepts, the "context-resource orthogonality" (Fig. 2.3), which asso-

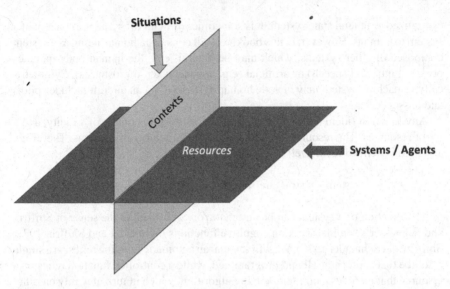

Fig. 2.3 The "context-resource orthogonality" framework

ciates the various resources, as systems, being considered in a variety of situations that induce contexts.

Indeed, when a system is designed (e.g., in the engineering sense) or observed (e.g., in the biological sense), it must be described in order to talk about it! It is most often described in the form of scenarios (e.g., stories or texts) that are both procedural (e.g., chronologies of events, scripts) and declarative (e.g., agents, actors, objects, places). In all cases, these scenarios need two basic ingredients:

- contexts to describe generic situations; and
- resources to ensure interactions in various relevant contexts.

The hyperspace of contexts constantly intersects with the hyperspace of resources. We need to make explicit (i.e., formalize) these contexts and resources together with their interconnections. This is what writers of novels or plays do. We can extend this approach to systems design. This is precisely what Brenda Laurel had already proposed when she described the use of computers, considering human-computer interaction as a play (Laurel 2013).

2.3 How Do Resources Work?

The resource concept cannot be properly considered without a system of systems approach (Popper et al. 2004) or a multi-agent approach (Wooldridge 2009). Indeed, a system, in the sense of systems engineering, or an agent, in the sense of artificial intelligence, can only work through the use of its internal or external resources that are systems, or agents. These resources, as systems, will also be able to work through their own internal or external resources, and so on. A resource can be passive or active. We will qualify a resource as an object in the first case, and as a subject in the second. The functional distinction "passive-active" translates into a systemic distinction "object-subject."

An object can be any cognitive or physical entity, natural or artificial. A subject may act or react and may be responsible for his/her/its actions. A subject can, and most often must, have situational awareness and the authority to act. The question of authority raises the question of responsibility. For example, the postman, responsible for delivering letters as a subject of the Post Office—we talk about a postal agent— uses a particular resource object, a bag that enables carrying the letters the postman has to deliver. This bag, as an object, does not engage any a priori responsibility, except when it becomes defective, in which case we will have to find out who made it and so on. We then deal with traceability and accountability. It is therefore clear that a subject resource may need subject resources and/or object resources, internal or external, which themselves may have subject resources and/or object resources, and so on. For example, in the case of a strike, the postman in charge (i.e., responsible for distributing a set of letters) may rely on temporary workers (i.e., subject resources) that he/she will have to train and supervise.

A subject resource is an entity that produces activity in response to the execution of a task. It must be equipped with processes for acquiring information (e.g., sensors, interpretation of information), adequate inference capabilities (e.g., procedures, rules, decision making), and performing actions (e.g., planning, actuators). Rasmussen's model provides an excellent framework for expressing these three cognitive processes (i.e., situational awareness, decision, and action) at different levels of behavior (e.g., subconscious or stimulus-response skills, automatic conscious rules, and conscious controlled knowledge). Interestingly, in well-known limited contexts, a subject-machine resource, such as the Flight Management System (FMS) onboard transport aircraft, has a rule-based behavior, such as described by Jens Rasmussen (1983).

Donald Norman provided an alternative to Rasmussen's model that supports emotional/cognitive design (Norman 2002, 2003). This model is used here to illustrate tangibility factors in contemporary design: visceral, behavioral and reflective. Figure 2.4 shows how Rasmussen's and Norman's models match.

In design, the visceral level is related to the look, feel and sound of things. It is directly related to physical tangibility. The behavioral level is related to the way systems work. It is about enjoyment and efficiency of use. The reflective level relates to the message, the physics and culture of the environment, and the meaning involved in using the system. According to Norman, the visceral level provides direct subconscious responses and provokes initial reactions (e.g., "I want it! It looks good too!"). The behavioral level provides conscious responses and leads to routine activities (e.g., "I can control it! It makes me feel smart!") The reflective level provides explanations (e.g., "It completes me! I can tell stories about it and myself!").

What are the design implications of Norman's model? At the visceral level, people are unconsciously looking for look-and-feel means, for example. Therefore, form

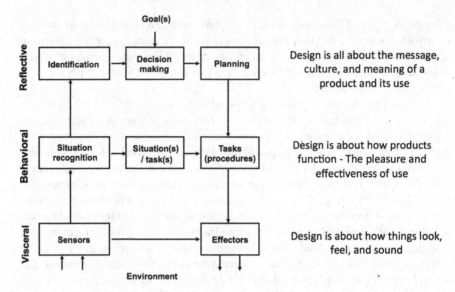

Fig. 2.4 The tangibility factors in contemporary design: an interpretation that combines the Rasmussen and Norman models

matters. It's about physical tangibility. Designers need to think about providing simple ideas, cues and directions. At the behavioral level, people need to be aware of the situation. Their conscious responses are guided by rules. This is both physical and figurative tangibility. Designers need to think about organizing things for routine cognitive work. At the level of reflection, people consciously search for meaning and culture. Therefore, appropriate explanations and visualizations are important. This is figurative tangibility, where it is crucial to make things explicit. Designers must think about providing humanly understandable support in real time.

A resource can be reactive, proactive, and/or social. A thermostat, for example, is a reactive resource that maintains a constant temperature in a room. GPS is a proactive navigation resource that provides geographic directions to the driver, based on a goal to be achieved. Some navigation systems, such as Waze, are fed in real time by information coming from other drivers on road conditions, making it a social resource. In all cases, there is a progression from the reactive to the social via the proactive, the social including the proactive, which includes the reactive. It is clear that reactive resources are generally thought of, developed and used as single-agent systems. At the other end of the spectrum, social resources can only be thought of, built and put into activity as multi-agent systems. In the middle, proactive resources can be cognitive systems, usually multi-agent systems.

2.4   Towards a Contextual Model of Situation Awareness

We have seen that HSI leads to the context-resource orthogonality framework (Fig. 2.3). It is time to better define the notion of context, which is closely linked to that of the situation. If we refer to the philosopher Joëlle Zask's analysis of the distinction between "context" and "situation" by John Dewey (Backe 1999), "a situation is an outcome and a context is a prerequisite" (Zask 2008). The notion of situation is associated with that of the environment in which the action is carried out. Here we link the notion of context to that of persistence (Boy 1998). Indeed, when a situation lasts in a certain space and for a certain time, we say that we are in a certain context. For example, the commentator of a rugby match may talk about the "context of the game," to refer to characteristics of the two teams, what has just happened since the start of the match, the shape of certain players, etc. Everything that follows will be interpreted in relation to this prerequisite. The notion of situation takes place at the action level. We will talk about à failure situation (i.e., an unfortunate result) for example.

The notion of context can be considered from various points of view. In this book focused on systems engineering and, more specifically, HSI, context is considered as a space defined by three kinds of factors: structure, function, and dynamics. When a system is being designed and developed, the context of the validity of this system must be clearly defined. First, this context of validity is made of structural parts. For example, when an onboard system is being designed for an aircraft, several structural parts can be considered, such as flight quality handling, navigation, collision avoidance and weather conditions. Some of these structural parts may not be considered for simplification purposes. For example, if the weather conditions are not considered, the context will be defined without considering weather conditions. Second, the context of validity is also made of functional parts. In addition, the functionalities of a new onboard system will necessarily depend on the structural parts being defined. For example, the TCAS (Traffic-alert Collision Avoidance System) relies on technical capabilities as well as human functions that should be activated at the right time. Third, the context of validity is also made of dynamics parts. For example, if the pilot executes a task in a wrong order or misses an action, then the dynamics context will not be what is usually expected. Summing up, context should be defined considering structural, functional and dynamic aspects.

This structure/function/dynamics context framework should be put in perspective with two other context frameworks: engineering/operations and technology/organization/people (see the TOP model in Fig. 3.3). Figure 2.5 provides a global framework for context analysis.

In practice, we will often use the terms "context" and "situation" interchangeably in this book, clarifying certain aspects that differentiate them when necessary. The first of these aspects to be clarified is context, which can be seen as a situational pattern (i.e., a set of persistent structured states according to certain conditions), such as the various phases of flight of an aircraft that is clearly defined as contexts. All pilots know how these contexts (e.g., phases of flight) are structured in space

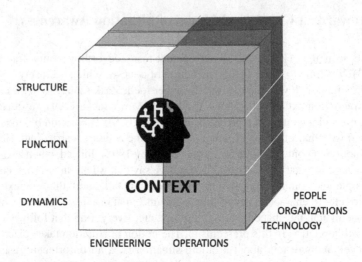

Fig. 2.5 Contextual framework for HSI

and time and how they are related to each other. All of these contexts establish an environment in which several situations can be described. For example, in the phase of flight "taxi to take-off", there are the situations "release brakes," "V1 decision speed beyond which one can no longer stop," and "VR take-off speed" which delimit (sub-) contexts.

When we speak of a context-sensitive system, this means that it has a mechanism of situation awareness (SA) in Mica Endsley's sense (1995), as a sequence of three high-level cognitive functions: perception, comprehension and projection. This cognitive mechanism of perceiving, interpreting and projecting the external situation is, in fact, only part of the problem (Endsley 1995; Endsley and Garland 2000; Boy 2015). Figure 2.6 shows an extension in these mechanisms by considering several types of situations, or situational patterns.

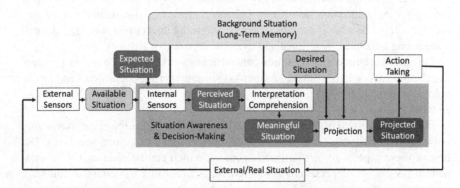

Fig. 2.6 Contextual model of situation awareness

It is useful to distinguish between intrinsic and extrinsic situations: an intrinsic situation concerns states, or factors, internal to an agent or system (e.g., individual's workload, awareness, decision-making, etc.); an extrinsic situation concerns states, or factors, external to an agent or system (e.g., atmospheric conditions, information sent by another agent or system, etc.).

The concept of situation has several interconnected facets (Fig. 2.6): the "real situation"; the "available situation"; the "perceived situation"; the "expected situation"; the "meaningful situation"; the "desired situation"; the "background situation" and the "projected situation."

The "real situation" is characterized by an infinite number of intimately interconnected states, some of which are not accessible to us, either because there is no mechanism that makes them accessible or because we do not know if they exist at all (e.g., many states describing the evolution of the market are not directly available to traders).

The "available situation" is characterized by a set of states accessible to a human observer through external sensors (e.g., physically measured variables, human-supplied key performance indicators, market development states accessible to traders); note that this is a subset of the "real situation."

The "perceived situation" is a subset of the "available situation," directed, augmented and/or transformed by what is expected (i.e., the "expected situation") and the agent's long-term memory (i.e., the "memory situation"); it is obtained from internal sensors (e.g., eyes, hearing, gesture sensors); visualization techniques, developed in the field of human-computer interaction for example, can improve the perceived situation.

The "expected situation" serves as a support for event-driven behavior (i.e., what we anticipate); the more a situation is expected, the more likely it is to be actually perceived. Conversely, any unexpected situation will be more difficult to be perceived. However, when people expect an event to happen with great confidence, they may get confused and mix up the "perceived situation" with the "expected situation." In fact, there is a huge difference between monitoring and control activities. People involved in a monitoring activity are usually guided by an objective and their process of situational awareness is oriented by the task they have to perform (i.e., their role in the context they are in). Conversely, people who only have to monitor a process have to use, and sometimes construct in real time, an artificial monitoring process that can be difficult, boring and sometimes irrelevant; in this case, the situational awareness process is likely to be performed incorrectly.

The "meaningful situation" is an interpretation of the "perceived situation" influenced by the "desired situation" (i.e., what we want to do) and the background situation (i.e., driven by experience and habits). We are in the presence of an interpretation process that leads to a model, scenarios or a polysemic picture of the situation. Moreover, the meaningful situation is dynamic (i.e., human operators gradually construct their own mental models or mental images of the situation). The resulting mental image depends on people, cultural context, ongoing activities and other factors specific to the field under study.

The "desired situation" expresses goal-oriented behavior (e.g., what we want to get out of what is happening in the current situation). Understanding what is happening is useful and necessary for doing the right thing, and another set of conditions must be established.

The "projected situation" can then be seen as the result of an inference process based on the meaningful situation supplemented by the background situation (e.g., immediate experience and long-term habits).

The "background situation" results from appropriate reminders in the long-term memory, based on expert knowledge.

It must also be taken into account that the real situation is impacted by the actions carried out and returns into the external sensor circuit. This situational loop is alive and cannot be considered statically, but rather dynamically. This is what the contextual model of SA is about.

2.5 Conclusion

This chapter provided a framework for flexibility analysis where the shift from rigid automation to flexible autonomy requires a consistent systemic representation. In other words, the concept of system is considered as a representation composed of a structure and a function. In addition, a system can be a resource for other systems in appropriate contexts. Two conceptual frameworks have been proposed: the context-resource orthogonality; and a contextual model of SA. Design for flexibility also belongs to the HSI emergent discipline that will be further described in the next chapter.

References

Backe A (1999) Dewey and the reflex arc: the limits of James's influence. Trans Charles S Peirce Soc 35(2):312–326

Boy GA (2020) Human systems integration: from virtual to tangible. CRC, Taylor and Francis, Boca Raton, FL, USA

Boy GA (2015) On the complexity of situation awareness. In: Proceedings 19th triennial congress of the IEA, Melbourne, Australia, pp 9–14

Boy GA (2013) Orchestrating human-centered design. Springer, U.K.

Boy GA (1998) Cognitive function analysis. Praeger/Ablex, USA. ISBN 9781567503777

Endsley MR, Garland DJ (eds) (2000) Situation awareness analysis and measurement. Lawrence Erlbaum Associates, Mahwah, NJ

Endsley MR (1995) Toward a theory of situation awareness in dynamic systems. Human Fact J Human Fact Ergon Soc 37(1):32–64

Klochko VE (2007) The logic of the development of psychological knowledge and the problem of the method of science. Methodol Hist Psychol 2(1):5–19

Laurel B (2013) Computers as theatre. Addison-Wesley Professional. ISBN-13:978-0321918628

Norman DA (2002) Emotion and design: attractive things work better. Interact Mag 4:36–42

Norman DA (2003) Emotional design: why we love (or hate) everyday things. Basic Books. ISBN-13: 978-0465051359

Popper S, Bankes S, Callaway R, DeLaurentis D (2004) System-of-systems symposium: report on a summer conversation. Potomac Institute for Policy Studies, Arlington, VA

Rasmussen J (1983) Skills, rules, knowledge; signals, signs and symbols, and other distinctions in human performance models. IEEE Trans Syst Man Cybern 13:257–266

Schneider W, Shiffrin RM (1977) Controlled and automatic human information processing: I. Detection, search, and attention. Psychol Rev 84(1):1–66. https://doi.org/10.1037/0033-295X.84.1.1

Shiffrin RM, Schneider W (1977) Controlled and automatic human information processing: II. perceptual learning, automatic attending and a general theory. Psychol Rev 84(2):127–190. https://doi.org/10.1037/0033-295x.84.2.127

Taleb NN (2007) The black swan: the impact of the highly improbable. Random House, New York. ISBN 978-1-4000-6351-2

Wooldridge M (2009) An introduction to multi-agent systems. Wiley. ISBN: 978-0470519462

Zask J (2008) Situation ou contexte? Une lecture de Dewey. Revue Internationale de Philosophie, No 245, pp. 313–328. https://www.cairn.info/revue-internationale-de-philosophie.htm

Chapter 3
A Few Methodological Clarifications

Abstract Design for flexibility requires some methodological clarifications in terms of underlying models. The SFAC model (Structure/Function vs. Abstract/Concrete) provides an abstract and concrete articulation between the structure and function of system. A sociotechnical system cannot be studied, modeled, designed and developed if the distinction and complementarity of cognitive and physical functions, which characterize it, are not well mastered. The NAIR (Natural/Artificial vs. Cognitive/Physical) model rationalizes this distinction to support human-centered design. The AUTOS pyramid (Artifact, User, Task, Organization and Situation) is an extension of the TOP model (Technology, Organization and People). SFAC, NAIR and AUTOS models and frameworks enable a design team to rationally state design problems toward enhanced HSI.

3.1 What Are Complex Sociotechnical Systems?

In this book, we consider the notion of system as a generic representation, or model, of a natural (e.g., a human being, an animal, a plant) or artificial (e.g., a human-made object, a machine) entity. We are interested in systems that integrate humans and machines, which we refer to interchangeably as "complex sociotechnical systems," "human–machine systems," "complex systems," or "sociotechnical systems" (Grudin 1994; Carayon 2006; Baxter and Sommerville 2010; Norman and Stappers 2016).

In general, a complex system can be characterized by the following properties:

- a large number of components and interconnections between these components;
- many people involved in its life cycle, which includes design, development, manufacturing, operation, maintenance and dismantling;
- emerging global properties and behaviors not included in the components;
- complex adaptive mechanisms and behaviors;
- non-linearities and possible chaos, which characterize its possible unpredictability.

Aircraft, industrial power plants and large defense systems are examples of complex systems. Their design, manufacture, use, repair and dismantling generally involve many financial and human resources.

In contrast, a simple system can be defined by the following properties:

- a small number of components and interconnections;
- behaviors directly related to the components;
- simple adaptive mechanisms and behaviors;
- linear or slightly near-linear responses to inputs.

A simple system is, for example, a coffee cup, a bicycle or a table. Its manufacture does not require the intervention of many people, except in the case of mass production.

From a design point of view, complexity must be addressed from both a structural point of view (i.e., structure of structures) and a functional point of view (i.e., function of functions). For example, the life cycle of an aircraft involves complex processes that involve a large number of complex systems that are structurally and functionally articulated. Therefore, it is necessary to articulate several trades to design and manufacture a complex system, such as an aircraft. There is no room for improvisation. Whether they are designers, manufacturers, maintainers or human operators at the end of the line, people who deal with complex systems need to become familiar with their complexity as well as with the environment in which they are immersed. This is what the analysis of sociotechnical systems complexity is all about.

Finally, Human-Centered Design (HCD) of complex systems is necessarily interdisciplinary, as no one person can make all possible contributions to the design of these systems, but a well-trained team can. For this reason, collaborative work is an important part of HCD (Poltrock and Grudin 2003). Theoretical models presented in this book are either chosen or constructed using my aerospace experience in dealing with complex systems.

The complexity of a system can be analyzed in a variety of ways depending on whether one is dealing with static or dynamic systems, as well as natural or artificial systems. Corresponding approaches can be based on different theories such as non-linear mathematical equations; fractals (Mandelbrot 1983); graphs; catastrophe theory (Thom 1989); and multi-agent systems (Wooldridge 2009). We will introduce three conceptual frameworks that will support flexibility in HCD (Boy 2017): the SFAC model; the NAIR model and the AUTOS pyramid.

3.2   The SFAC Model

To design an artifact (i.e., an artificial system, a machine) is to define its structure and function. Each structure and function can be described in both abstract and concrete terms. The SFAC model (Structure/Function vs. Abstract/Concrete) provides a double articulation (i.e., abstract and concrete) between the structure and function of an artifact (Fig. 3.1) as follows:

Fig. 3.1 The SFAC model
(Boy 2017)

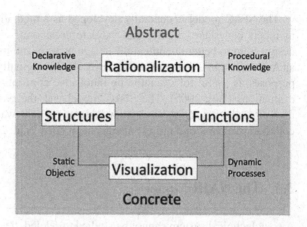

- declarative knowledge (i.e., abstract structures);
- procedural knowledge (i.e., abstract functions);
- static objects or systems (i.e., concrete structures); and
- dynamic processes (i.e., concrete functions).

The abstract part is a rationalization of the system being designed (i.e., knowledge representation). This rationalization can be formalized by a set of concepts linked together by relationships. This type of representation can be referenced as ontology, semantic network or concept map. It can take the form of a tree hierarchy in the simplest case, or a complex concept graph in most cases.

The terms "declarative" and "procedural" refer respectively to the "know-what" and the "knowhow." They are used to describe human memory. Declarative memory includes facts and defines our own semantics of things. Procedural memory includes skills and procedures (i.e., how to do things). We can think of declarative memory as an explicit network of concepts. Procedural memory can be thought of as an implicit set of skills (i.e., constituting knowhow). We hypothesize that the cortex is composed of declarative memory and procedural memory evolving through learning. The former is generally stored in the temporal cortex of the brain. The second is stored in the motor cortex. These concepts are used in the PRODEC method described in this book.

According to the SFAC model, at the design stage, the physical part is usually represented using Computer-Aided Design (CAD) software, which enables the designer to generate 3D models of various components of the system being designed. These 3D models include static objects and dynamic processes that visualize how the components being designed work and are integrated together. Later in the design and development process, these 3D models can be printed in 3D, which gives a more concrete—we will say physically tangible—picture of the components being built and their possible integration. Testing takes place at each stage of the design process by considering together the concrete parts and their abstract counterparts (i.e., their rationalization, justifications and the various relationships that exist between them).

The SFAC model is generally developed as a mediation space that design-team members can share, modify and validate collaboratively. SFAC also enables the design team to better document the design process and its solutions. The concept of an Active Design Document (ADD) (Boy 1997), originally developed for traceability purposes, is useful for streamlining innovative concepts and progressive formative evaluations (Boy 2005). The SFAC model was the basis of the SCORE system used as mediation support to a team designing a light-water nuclear reactor, in their collaborative work and project management (Boy et al. 2016).

3.3 The NAIR Model

A sociotechnical system cannot be studied, modeled, designed and developed if the distinction and complementarity of cognitive and physical functions, which characterize it, are not well mastered. The NAIR (Natural/Artificial vs. Cognitive/Physical) model rationalizes this distinction to support human-centered design (Fig. 3.2).

Natural systems include biological systems (e.g., plants, animals and people), and physical systems (e.g., geological or atmospheric phenomena). Artificial systems include cognitive systems (e.g., Internet, digital watches and aircraft flight management systems), and physical systems (e.g., houses, bridges and factories).

Rationalist philosophies can be used to explain natural intentional behavior (i.e., primarily related to the cortex, including reasoning, understanding and learning). Vitalist philosophies can be used to explain reactive behavior (i.e., primarily related to emotions, experience, and skills).

Artificial intelligence tools and techniques can be used to support the generation of artificial intentional behavior (e.g., operations research, optimization techniques and knowledge-based systems). Control theories and human–machine interaction tools and techniques can be used to support the generation of artificial reactive behavior

Fig. 3.2 The NAIR model (Boy 2017)

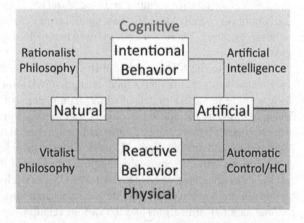

(e.g., aircraft traffic alert and collision avoidance systems, control mechanisms and voice output to generate alarms to pilots).

3.4 The TOP Model

Designing a new system necessarily involves people: people as designers first; people as developers and manufacturers; people as testers and certifiers; people as users or operators; people as maintenance operators and repairers; and finally, people as dismantling specialists. Starting with designers, how can we help them in their jobs? What tools, types of organization and qualifications do we need to deal with? Tools to support the acquisition and clarification of HCD requirements in terms of technology, organization and people involved (i.e., the TOP Model as illustrated in Fig. 3.3).

HCD has been developed for more than two decades (Norman 2019; Boy 2013). HCD emerged as a reaction to the rigid world of traditional engineering design, which puts the technological element before the human element; the latter is always taken into account too late through the development of user interfaces and operational documentation. In fact, HCD has its roots in Human–Computer Interaction (HCI), which takes into account human factors in computer systems and, for that matter, has also become a design discipline. Donald Norman is certainly one of the best promoters of HCD, where he recognized the need to observe the activity, differentiating between logic and usage, at design time. This led to the concept of user experience (Edwards and Kasik 1974; Norman 1988). The HCD encompasses what Norman (1986) calls User Centered System Design (UCSD). The term "user" can be misleading for two reasons. First, it suggests end users (e.g., pilots, drivers, control room operators) and not necessarily, for example, certifiers, maintainers and trainers. Second, the human beings who are included in a system are more than users; they are people!

For example, the NASA Human Systems Integration Practitioner's Guide provides a very clear and explicit definition of HCD in space (NASA 2015):

1. Concepts of operations and scenario development;
2. Task analysis;

Fig. 3.3 The TOP model (Boy 2013)

Fig. 3.4 The AUT triangle

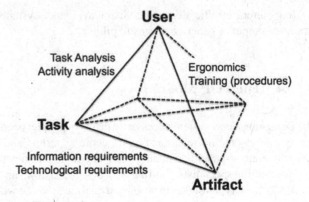

3. Distribution of functions between humans and systems;
4. Distribution of roles and responsibilities among humans;
5. Iterative conceptual design and prototyping;
6. Empirical testing, for example, testing with a representative population, or model-based assessment of human and system performance;
7. In situ monitoring of human–system performance in flight.

3.5   The AUTO Pyramid

The AUTOS pyramid[1] (Artifact, User, Task, Organization and Situation) is an extension of the TOP model (Fig. 3.3). It is a framework for streamlining HCD and engineering. The AUT triangle (Fig. 3.4) describes three edges: task and activity analysis (U-T); information requirements and technological limitations (T-A); ergonomics and training (procedures) (T-U).

For example, artifacts can be systems, devices and parts of aircraft or consumer electronics. Users may be novices, experienced personnel, or experts, from and within various cultures. They may be tired, stressed, make mistakes, old or young, and in very good shape and spirits. Tasks range from managing handling qualities to flight management, managing a passenger cabin, designing or repairing a system, supplying or managing a team or organization. Each task involves one or more cognitive functions that users concerned must learn and use.

The organizational environment includes all the natural or artificial systems that interact with the user performing the task while using the artifact (Fig. 3.5). It introduces three other aspects: social issues (U-O); role and task analysis (T-O); and emergence and evolution (A-O).

---

[1] The AUTOS Pyramid was described in detail in the introduction to the Handbook of Human–Machine Interaction (Boy 2011). It should be noted that the term "user" is used in this model to denote a human interacting with a machine, itself denoted as an "artifact." We keep these denotations to ensure the continuity of the AUTOS model, designed in the context of human–computer interaction and used here in the context of human-system integration.

Fig. 3.5 The AUTO tetrahedron

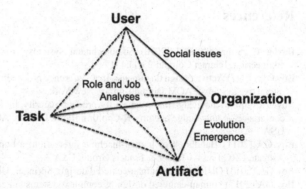

Fig. 3.6 The AUTO pyramid

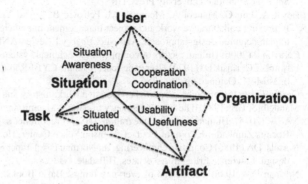

The AUTOS framework, also called the AUTOS pyramid (Fig. 3.6), is an extension of the AUTO tetrahedron introducing a new dimension, the "situation," which has been implicitly included in the "organizational environment". The three new aspects are: usability/usefulness (A-S); situation awareness (U-S); situated actions (T-S); cooperation/coordination (O-S).

The AUTOS pyramid is a useful support for human-centered designers in the analysis, design and evaluation of HSI, taking into account human factors, artifactual factors and integrative factors that combine task factors, organizational factors and situational factors.

3.6 Conclusion

Three conceptual models, SFAC, NAIR and AUTOS Pyramid, are useful for human-centered design teams to better understand and master the meaning of and relationships between system's structures and functions, concrete and abstract things, physical and cognitive agents, natural and artificial entities, as well as an artifact, task, user, organization and situation concepts.

References

Baxter G, Sommerville I (2010) Sociotechnical systems: from design methods to systems engineering. Interact Comput 23(1):4–17

Boy GA (1997) Active design documents. In: Conference proceedings of ACM DIS'93 (Designing interactive systems). ACM Digital Library, New York, USA

Boy GA (2005) Knowledge management for product maturity. In: Proceedings of the international conference on knowledge capture (K-Cap'05), Banff, Canada. ACM Digital Library, New York, USA

Boy GA (2011) Handbook of human-machine interaction: a human-centered design approach. Ashgate/CRC Press—Taylor & Francis Group, USA

Boy GA (2013) Orchestrating human-centered design. Springer, UK

Boy GA (2017) Human-centered design of complex systems: an experience-based approach. Des Sci J 3. Cambridge University Press, UK

Boy GA, Jani G, Manera A, Memmott M, Petrovic B, Rayad Y, Stephane AL, Suri N (2016) Improving collaborative work and project management in a nuclear power plant design team: a human-centered design approach. Ann Nucl Energy Elsevier. ANE4864

Carayon P (2006) Human factors of complex sociotechnical systems. Appl Ergon 37(4):525–535

Edwards EC, Kasik DJ (1974) User experience with the CYBER graphics terminal. In: Proceedings of VIM-21, October, pp. 284–286

Grudin J (1994) Computer-supported cooperative work: history and focus. Computer 27(5):19–26

Mandelbrot BB (1983) The fractal geometry of nature, Macmillan. ISBN:978-0-7167-1186-5

NASA (2015) Human systems integration (HSI) Practitioner's guide. NASA/SP-2015-3709. Rochlis Zumbado, J. Point of Contact. Johnson Space Center, Houston, TX

Norman DA (1986) Cognitive engineering. In: Norman DA, Draper SW (eds) User centered system design. Lawrence Erlbaum Associates, Hillsdale, NJ

Norman DA (1988) The design of everyday things. Basic Books, New York. ISBN 978-0-465-06710-7

Norman DA (2019) The four fundamental principles of human-centered design and application. Essay (retrieved on June 29, 2020: https://jnd.org/the-four-fundamental-principles-ofhuman-cen tered-design/)

Norman D, Stappers PJ (2016) DesignX: design and complex sociotechnical systems. She Ji J Des Econ Innov 1(2):83–106. https://doi.org/10.1016/j.sheji.2016.01.002

Poltrock SE, Grudin J (2003) Collaboration technology in teams, organizations, and communities. Tutorial. CHI'2003 Conference. ACM Digital Library (http://www.chi2003.org/docs/t13.pdf)

Thom R (1989) Structural stability and morphogenesis: an outline of a general theory of models. Addison-Wesley, Reading, MA. ISBN: 0-201-09419-3

Wooldridge M (2009) An introduction to multi-agent systems, 2nd edn. Wiley. ISBN: 978-0470519462

Chapter 4
Articulating Human Systems Integration

Abstract Human-centered design (HCD) has become effectively possible when human-in-the-loop simulation (HITLS) capabilities have emerged with the tremendous development of the twenty-first century's digital capabilities. Simulation enables us to holistically integrate people and systems. Interconnectivity in our digital society created new kinds of complexity and properties of complex systems, which need to be addressed, such as separability. HCD, supported by HITLS from the beginning of the design process by developing virtual prototypes of the target system, enables activity analysis, human-centered agile development and certification. Human systems integration (HSI) is the result of an appropriate mix of HCD and Systems Engineering (SE) during the whole lifecycle of a system. It can be considered as a field of investigation and even a new discipline. Therefore, human and organizational factors in the design of sociotechnical systems open epistemological issues and solutions. Finally, the shift from traditional engineering to digital engineering induces the shift from rigid automation to flexible autonomy, which involves artificial intelligence methods and tools based on the acquisition of procedural and declarative knowledge from experts. The PRODEC method enables such acquisition and will be presented.

4.1 Towards an Epistemology[1] of Human–System Integration

Now that the context-resource orthogonality framework has been defined and described as the central framework for human systems integration (HSI), it is time to present the current epistemological evolution induced by the development of HSI. At the beginning of the twenty-first century, HSI became a field of scientific and technical investigation in its own right (Pew and Marvor 2007; Pew 2008; Boehm-Davis et al. 2015; Boy 2020).

In this transitional period, traditional corrective ergonomics is giving way to the association of human-centered design with complex systems engineering towards

---

[1]Epistemology is the branch of philosophy concerned with the theory of knowledge. It studies the nature of knowledge, the justification and rationality of beliefs.

G. A. Boy, *Design for Flexibility*, Human–Computer Interaction Series,
https://doi.org/10.1007/978-3-030-76391-6_4

HSI (Boy and Narkevicius 2013). It is supported by interaction design developed by human–computer interaction. This new discipline in gestation is based on virtual prototyping, human-in-the-loop simulations (HITLS), and the development of tangibility metrics. The human element is now taken into account during the design process with the support of virtual spaces allowing activity analysis (in addition to task analysis), to test not just human–machine interfaces but the entire technical system being designed.

Human-centered engineering design involves multidisciplinary teams. If we are talking about humanizing technology, it is not about developing robots that look exactly like us (i.e., the great humanoid replacement), but about developing tools that are humanly and ecologically sound (i.e., that are not likely to defile nature or handicap our lives).

Moreover, the break that is taking place before our eyes directly addresses the traditional vision of two distinct sectors: research and practice. Thinking and doing are moving towards an integrated sociotechnical approach, HSI. It must be noted that technology is developing much faster than research can rationalize it. Today, the laboratory has become the real world. HSI integrates disciplines such as anthropology, ergonomics and architecture with engineering sciences and computer science.

HSI, as an anthropological approach, needs a solid philosophical foundation. The engineering sciences are largely based on positivism (Comte 1998; Russell 1993) and behaviorism (Watson 1913; Pavlov 1927; Skinner 1953), where consciousness is not observable, and therefore investigations of consciousness are close to metaphysics. Positivism is interested in everything that is observable. It leads to empiricism. Although HSI is strongly based on observation, it is also interested in phenomenology, introspection and the human experience (Heidegger 1927; Bergson 1907; Merleau-Ponty 1964). As HSI works in concert with systems engineering, the main question is: how to benefit from positivism without losing the meaning of what we are building? There is no answer to this question without a model or theory, as well as good practice. This is why theories of human cognition are very useful as mediation tools for observing problems, managing knowledge, and above all, taking experience into account. It is obvious that these theories need to be extended, especially in the field of socio-cognition.

HSI is necessarily based on models, to make simulations and to develop metrics (tangibility in particular). Each model evolves as it is used. A model is a set of elements that partially reproduces another set of richer elements that are commonly called "reality." We have seen how to give meaning to the concept of the situation by distinguishing, among other things, the perceived situation from the real situation. Several models can reproduce the same reality. These models can be concrete and/or abstract. An airplane can be modeled by a physical model, a drawing or a mathematical model. A good model is a useful model. A model is useful when the operations it represents and simulates make sense compared to equivalent operations in the real world.

To do this, one must choose the elements that make up the model and their interrelationships, to best represent the equivalent elements of the corresponding real world. In doing so, the systemic breakdown remains extremely difficult to identify

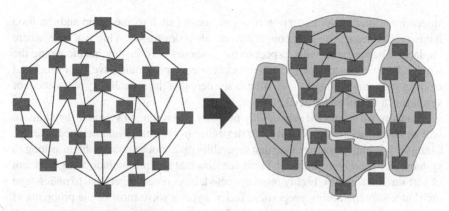

Fig. 4.1 Example of seven separable systems of a system of systems

because the real world is not strictly separable into pieces by the simple fact that the natural elements are part of a living chain that is necessarily interconnected. The Internet now shows us that we have recreated artificial systems with similar properties. Cutting the world into pieces and connecting them again to reconstruct an equivalent world is a matter for positivist mechanics, but not, generally speaking, a matter of human–system integration in the phenomenological sense.

This leads to the problem of systemic separability (Fig. 4.1). Indeed, the more complex[2] a system is, both structurally and functionally, the more difficult it is to apprehend its behavior and understand its internal functioning (i.e., the interactions between the various components of a system of systems).

Can parts of the system be separated to study them in isolation and thus simplify the analysis? This is a difficult question, but one that biologists and physiologists have been considering and studying for a long time. Surgeons, for example, know how to momentarily separate an organ from the human body without irreversibly damaging the whole body, considered as a system of systems. They also know that certain organs, such as the brain, cannot be separated because the human being could die from this separation. These vital organs must be studied and treated while being connected to the rest of the body.

The traditional silo system design approach that leads to late integration of system components most often leads to major problems that are difficult, and even impossible, to deal with at the end of the chain because rebuilding the entire system is difficult and at times impossible. This approach does not consider the property of separability and considers that all the components of a system are separable, like Lego blocks.

For example, a country may be separable with respect to some parameters and not with respect to others. More specifically, during the COVID-19 pandemic, the French government decided to lock down the whole population instead of locking down the severely infected regions by the virus. It resulted that the whole country

---

[2]Complex is taken in the Latin sense of "complexus," i.e. what is woven together (Morin 1995).

stopped working to the exception of a few sectors such as medicine and the food industry. Consequently, the economy went down drastically. This is a case where the lack of separability with respect to the economy was terribly handicapping the whole system, and separability with respect to geography could have been beneficial from an economic point of view. We can see here that the separability of a system of systems is a useful and crucial concept.

The more we master the separability property of a system of systems, the more we will be able to address its fluidity and flexibility in operations and maintenance, for example. It is important to realize that separability was not a major problem as long as systems were purely mechanical. However, now that systems include a large amount of software and are also highly interconnected, it becomes imperative to understand their intrinsic separability properties. Today, experts solve most of the problems of these complex sociotechnical systems, often using prosthetic devices, but we need to better formalize them, systemically speaking, to enable better mastery.

We have seen that any human or machine system can be represented by a structure and a function. A system of systems is itself an organization. Ilkka Tuomi made a distinction between the concepts of organization and structure. "Organization defines a class of systems, while structure is a particular implementation of a system in an organizational class" (Tuomi 1999, page 150). These systems not only evolve during their life cycle (i.e., they adapt in a homeostatic way), but they can also reproduce themselves in the sense of autopoiesis (self-procreation), a concept proposed by Maturana and Varela (1980). Tuomi proposed the 5-A model of knowledge generation that encapsulates knowledge generation: anticipation, appropriation, articulation, accumulation and action.

Imagine that an Internet server failure occurs and lasts for quite a long time. A number of difficult problems will arise. We have become dependent on this networked computer technology. Our lives depend on it! As a result of the COVID-19 break-down, we have to learn how to manage our lives differently. Information technology has created an organizational automation within which we have had to adapt. It is interesting to note that for all those whose work depended heavily on this type of technology, the COVID-19 pandemic not only did not disrupt them, but also enabled them to be more productive. During COVID-19, computer-supported meeting environments greatly supported remote working for some of us. In contrast, people who have had to ensure the physical survival of all of us have had to risk contamination. They have distinguished themselves from everyone else. They are working in health care, food production and distribution, vital manual labor and many other sectors.

We have to realize the extent to which the cognitive work of some people, whose medium is computers, cannot exist without the physical work of others, who live in the physical tangible world. In the post-COVID-19 phase, all these observations lead us to ask ourselves the central issue of tangibility, which itself opens up the field posed by the need for autonomy. We were able, in France for example, to become aware of this need for autonomy through the fact that we knew how to produce planes, but not masks, to protect each other from the pandemic. Airplanes were of no use to us, except to spread the pandemic more rapidly from around the world. During the spring of 2020, France's inability to produce masks and to have tests available led our fellow citizens to be confined for 2 months, in a directive and rigid manner. This is one of the important reasons why we need to rethink our economic system and the associated industrial system. In particular, the need for autonomy and flexibility, which becomes paramount in times of crisis, must be thought out in everyday life to ensure its sustainability.

4.2 Simulation Enables Us to Holistically Integrate People and Systems

Simulation has been around for decades, but now it is ubiquitous (i.e., we can connect here and now any kind of virtual system available somewhere else with almost no pain, no matter what sector). We can simulate in a very tangible way aerospace, nuclear or medical systems, for example. Tangibility will have to be better defined, of course. This book will provide a contribution on tangibility issues and approaches.

Nowadays, simulation provides central support in engineering design. It is strongly based on modeling, in the sense of computer-aided design (CAD) and dynamic system modeling. CAD was initially static, mainly based on finite element methods and partial differential equations, guiding decision-making for shape design. Today, simulation integrates all kinds of models, such as aerodynamics models, structural models, vibration models and so on. Simulation is progressively becoming multi-physical. In addition, we incrementally realized that simulation has a great influence on modeling. Finally, simulation has become easier to implement and affordable in terms of costs.

Most interesting, it enables the development of a human-in-the-loop simulation that provides invaluable support for virtual human-centered design (VHCD). It enables us to observe and test the activity of people involved in future systems. It enables formative evaluation of systems being designed and developed because we can observe the behavior of these systems and their environments in a holistic way. This was not possible before, and we could only test parts of a system, not the whole thing. Now, we can test the digital twin of the targeted system.

In twentieth century technology-centered engineering, everything was physical from the outset, resource commitments were also set at the outset, which severely limited design options (Fig. 4.2). Under these conditions, design flexibility quickly becomes a problem because there are not enough resources to compensate for it, and knowledge about the system becomes fully available too late (i.e., when it is almost complete), and in many cases even worse during operations. The only resources we had were the so-called "user interface" and "operations procedures". In many cases, the user interface is often developed more to compensate for functional design flaws than to harmonize the allocation of functions between people and machines.

Instead, if we use HITLS from the outset (i.e., by designing and developing virtual prototypes of the target system), we can test and analyze activity and thus get to know the system during design and development (Fig. 4.3).

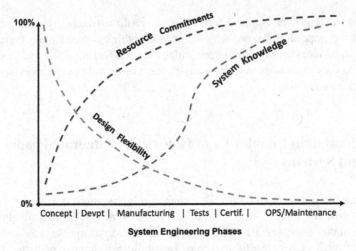

Fig. 4.2 Technology-centered resource commitments, design flexibility and system knowledge

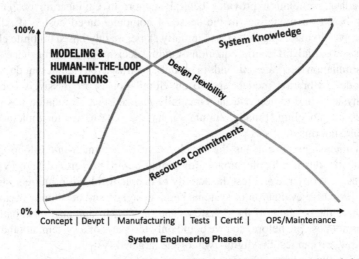

Fig. 4.3 Human-centered resource commitments, design flexibility and system knowledge

When a stakeholder asks, "what will it look like," we can show them the simulation and gain more knowledge about the system. This knowledge comes from usage (i.e., the activity generated using HITLS). You can better understand what needs to be changed. You still have options in resource management. You retain design flexibility.

Most important in the evolution of the three parameters (i.e., system knowledge, design flexibility and resource commitments) in relation to the life cycle of a system (i.e., systems engineering phases) is the consideration of all three at the same time (Fig. 4.3).

VHCD, as just described, based on HITLS, is done with the generation of large amounts of data that need to be processed. The use of artificial intelligence is often

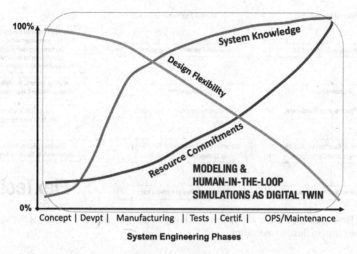

Fig. 4.4 Digital twin approach throughout the life cycle of a system

necessary for this type of processing. Emerging patterns must be extracted from this data. These patterns characterize emerging functions and structures of constantly evolving systems. This is often referred to as the agile approach. However, as long as we remain in the computer domain (i.e., in the domain of virtual prototypes), we are not completely in the realm of the tangible (Boy 2016), whether physical or figurative (cognitive). All this is new in engineering!

VHCD can be extended to the entire life cycle of the system under consideration. It should be noted that once a sociotechnical system is fully developed, virtual environments used to support the VHCD process can also be used and refined as digital twins (Fig. 4.4) to support operations and, in particular, the progressive integration of experience feedback. Figure 4.4 differs from Fig. 4.3 because the extension of "modeling and human-in-the-loop simulations" considered as a digital twin covers the entire life cycle of the system. In addition, a digital twin constitutes interactive documentation of the system. In maintenance, for example, a digital twin can be used to assist in troubleshooting and progressively integrate useful feedback information.

4.3 How Can More Autonomy and Flexibility Be Provided?

Traditional engineering (i.e., engineering based on techno-centric systems engineering) leads to automation, while digital engineering leads to human-centered systems design and, therefore, human systems integration (Fig. 4.5).

In today's traditional engineering, automation consists of introducing software into hardware. For example, a lot of software was introduced into automobiles at the end of the twentieth century, which allowed many human functions to be transferred to the machine. The machine functions produced were implemented by computerized

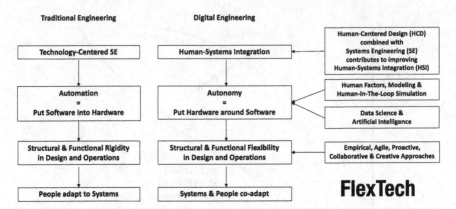

Fig. 4.5 How the shift from traditional engineering to digital engineering induces the shift from rigid automation to flexible autonomy

procedures and therefore rigid in the sense that when they are called upon, they do what they are programmed to do. Moreover, we find this rigidity in all the tools and processes of traditional engineering (in the quality sector, for example). This approach has led to an adaptation of the human being to the machine, even if we would like to make people believe that a human–machine interface enables us to do the opposite. In fact, in this type of engineering, the heart of the machine remains, and will remain, technology-centered.

In digital engineering, now called Industry 4.0, autonomy leads to automatically building hardware from software. For example, most systems begin to be designed on a computer: first a PowerPoint presentation is made, then a digital model is developed, and then a simulation that can be tested before any physically tangible hardware is developed. A complete aircraft can even be developed in the form of a video game simulating a very realistic aircraft; virtual flight tests can be implemented and allow for virtual business process analysis at an early stage in the life cycle of a system. It is precisely at this level that AI and data science can play a key role. In fact, they will enable the development of functions that will need to be optimally allocated to human or machine systems. It becomes crucial to ensure that, as much as possible, some of these functions can be allocated in a flexible and dynamic way (i.e., in real time). The analysis of cognitive functions enables us to better understand and decide on the construction and allocation of such functions, which most often emerge from the activity itself (Boy 1998, 2013, 2020). This human-centered approach leads to a co-adaptation of the human beings and machines concerned.

Why does flexibility become so important? It should be noted that we have not stopped building artifacts, substituting human functions by machine functions (i.e., by automating), especially in the aeronautics sector. Let's take Rasmussen's model to explain this recent evolution of automation towards a need for autonomy (Fig. 4.6).

In the aviation industry, it all started with the automation of basic skills such as maintaining speed and altitude. First aircraft autopilots were installed as early as the early 1930s. It is interesting to note that the corresponding technical and scientific disciplines developed concomitantly with the industrial development of the same

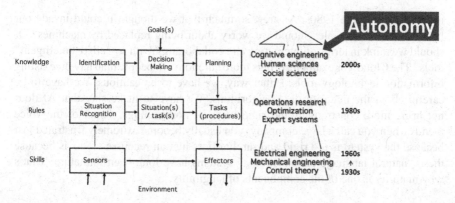

Fig. 4.6 Emergence of disciplines in the service of HCD in the quest for automation towards greater autonomy

objects and concepts. We might use the metaphor of industry being the university of reality. For example, the theory of cybernetics, developed by Norbert Wiener, flourished in the 1940s (Wiener 1948), long after the use of autopilots in commercial aviation. We can therefore give a time window between the 1930s and 1960s for the transition of skills-based functions, in Rasmussen's sense, from human to machine, using methods and tools developed by electrical engineering, mechanical engineering and control theories, more specifically automatic control.

It wasn't until the 1980s that the first digital computers arrived on board transport aircraft. The navigation system, the Flight Management System (FMS), was built in the mid-1980s through the development of a computer that calculates the optimal flight path in real time based on given waypoints. We had transferred the functions normally performed by pilots to the machine through computers managing air route databases. The FMS operates in a loop over the autopilot. Such systems were built using methods and tools from operational research, system optimization, and expert systems.

Cognitive engineering was born in the early 1980s in response to a need to integrate cognitive science and computer science for the development of human–computer interaction (Card et al. 1983; Norman 1986; Rasmussen 1983). Moreover, cognitive engineering was born at the height of artificial intelligence (1980s version!). At that time, cognitive science and AI had begun to work well together. The former provided a human substrate for the latter, and the latter offered models for the former, computer science being the test and measurement medium for these two disciplines. Unfortunately, this first wave of artificial intelligence (AI) did not bring the ambitious results expected and subsequently plunged into a harsh "winter" from the 1990s onwards. Human–computer interaction (HCI) then developed, being more pragmatic and offering tangible results in the much shorter term than AI (Winograd 2006; Grudin 2009; Kolski et al. 2020).

As far as AI is concerned, it is useful at this point to review what this discipline has become and really addresses. John McCarthy and Marvin Minsky presented the first artificial intelligence program in the Dartmouth Summer Research Project in 1956. During the 1980s, AI grew so much that we thought it could invade our lives and replace people. Should we worry about being replaced by machines? Or should we think in terms of interacting and collaborating with so-called "intelligent" tools? The Cloud, for example, brings more autonomy to people than any preexisting information technology tools. Either way, we have to be cautious. We have to be careful about the maturity of AI algorithms. We have to make sure that AI does not bring more constraining and rigid ways of doing things. Think of the voice menus when you call a large company; you usually become extremely frustrated just because the system is too rigid and rarely offers human recourses. This is because these "natural language understanding" systems have long been immature. That's why maturity is one of the components of tangibility.

4.4   Artificial Intelligence and Systems Engineering

We have already seen that the concept of an agent in AI is analogous to that of the system in Systems Engineering (SE). Therefore, it is no coincidence that a cross-fertilization of the two disciplines is gradually taking place. In this book, I recall once again that the terms agent, in the AI sense, and system, in the SE sense, are often used instead of each other. A "Multi-Agent System" (MAS) in AI is equivalent to a "System of Systems" (SoS) in SE.

The question of machine learning is still much discussed in order to better understand how to assimilate generic knowledge structures and how to accommodate the parameters they contain, in the Piaget's sense. It is clear that, in the first instance, learning will have to be supervised (by human beings, experts in the underlying domain). Several AI techniques emerged in the 1980s, such as case-based reasoning and associated learning mechanisms, which consist of making specific cases more generic. This type of induction mechanism is symbolic in nature. Time has passed, and AI has developed to strengthen fields of research and development such as robotics, the semantic Web, knowledge management and, more recently, data science (big data) as an extension of classical methods of numerical data analysis through the use of statistical mathematics. In the phases of upstream assimilation of generic models, human systems integration will be based more on symbolic than numerical AI methods. In the downstream accommodation phases, the use of numerical data will be done naturally for the functional adjustment of generic model parameters.

More and more AI algorithms are being implemented in systems for SE. This is what McDermott and colleagues refer to as AI4SE (i.e., Artificial Intelligence for Systems Engineering; McDermott et al. 2020).[3] A similar initiative took place in 2019 in Leganès, Spain, where the premises of this book were published (Boy

---

[3] In 2019, the Research Council of the Systems Engineering Research Center (SERC), a US Department of Defense sponsored by the University Affiliated Research Center (UARC), developed a roadmap to structure and guide research in artificial intelligence and autonomy. This roadmap includes key aspects of the underlying transformation of digital engineering both enabling the automation of traditional systems engineering (AI4SE) practices and encouraging new practices in systems engineering to support a new wave of automated, adaptive, and learning systems (SE4AI).

2019). This first colloquium focused on the contributions of AI to the field of SE (i.e., AI4SE). This trend follows the lines anticipated by Herbert Simon in the science of the artificial (Simon 1996).

What are the main topics currently being discussed in the AI community? The AAAI[4] 2020[5] conference proposed the following topics: information retrieval (search); planning; knowledge representation; reasoning; natural language processing; robotics and perception; multi-agent systems; statistical learning; and deep learning. In summary, current AI could be classified into two broad categories: data science and robotics.

However, AI should not only be based on human cognition but also on other forms of intelligence when it makes sense. Look at a flock of birds. Isn't it intelligent? A flock of birds, flying in close formation usually creates majestic and aerodynamically effective patterns. It's natural collective intelligence. Besides, look at the evolution of the species. Look at the interactions of individuals and groups within a community. Interactions within social groups, teams, communities and organizations have their own intelligence that is interesting to model and understand. This is why it is very important to have this kind of experience-based common sense about multi-agent systems, be they natural or artificial. Therefore, it is time to open up the concept of human systems integration, considering not only human cognition but more generally artificial life at the service of natural life, leading to more harmonious and symbiotic sociotechnical systems. Consequently, distributed AI (i.e., multi-agent approaches) and systems theory have much in common. AI researcher Marvin Minsky defined an agent as a society of agents (Minsky 1986). We inevitably return to the cross-fertilization of AI and SE.

Expertise and experience were widely studied in the late 1980s and 1990s, particularly in the area of knowledge acquisition for Knowledge-Based Systems (KBS) (Gaines and Boose 1988). Expert systems and rule-based systems belong to the class of KBS. This field of investigation has fostered a range of automation of expertise and experience. Unfortunately, it has declined over the years since the mid-1990s because it was not mature in terms of flexibility and support for creativity in the services it could provide (i.e., in most cases, people outperformed KBS because of KBS's lack of flexibility in problem solving).

For example, we have used KBS as support for experience feedback management in order to preserve and reuse knowledge about experience and expertise. Large knowledge bases have been developed, but they have rarely been used effectively and sustainably. Today, thanks to digital twin technology (i.e., numerical models and simulations of real-world systems) and supervised machine learning, we can progressively integrate, instead of accumulating, knowledge from experience feedback in a meaningful and usable way. Specifically, it is likely that digital twins will be used as operational support for troubleshooting, situational awareness, decision making and implementation of actions.

In this sense, AI has a bright future ahead of it to empower people at high cognitive levels (e.g., through supervised machine learning for the development of complex

[4]Association for the Advancement of Artificial Intelligence.
[5]https://aaai.org/Conferences/AAAI-20/aaai20call/.

system architectures), as well as more basic levels of behavior (e.g., through deep learning of vision and image recognition systems). In the first case, AI will be more symbolic, and in the second, it will be more based on algorithms for digital data mining and analysis.

Moving towards greater autonomy is a major challenge for our societies. Which models should we study? In any case, these models will strongly depend on context. This is why the concept of context is crucial and will need further research. Any model has to be built using more or less explicit rules. Even if these rules are difficult to write, they exist and define a community of practice. Expressionist and Cubist painters represent nature differently according to their technical choices of visualization. When these rules persist, the community becomes more structured and stronger. For example, new systems using artificial intelligence algorithms are being built to help fighter pilots in their tasks. What are the rules that must be followed to ensure trust and collaboration between pilots and these virtual assistants? The PRODEC approach has been developed with this in mind.

4.5   PRODEC[6]: Acquisition of Procedural and Declarative Knowledge

Human-centered design (HCD) of complex systems is a question of identifying the multiple human and machine entities, considered as systems, which may be physical and/or cognitive (cyber). We have seen in this book that they can be modeled by roles, contexts of validity and resources that are themselves systems. These properties must therefore be correctly identified. PRODEC is a method for this purpose. PRODEC is based on the distinction between procedural and declarative knowledge, made in computer science.

Procedural knowledge concerns the experience of operations, often expressed in the form of narratives by experts in the field. Declarative knowledge concerns the objects and agents involved in the human–machine system to be designed. The PRODEC method revolves around the acquisition of procedural knowledge from subject matter experts and elicitation of various properties and attributes of human and machine systems. This elicitation process is iterative and based on creativity, development and validation of prototypes. The PRODEC process can take several iterations to converge. It is strongly recommended to run simulations with humans in the loop to perform this validation and progressively create and maintain appropriate performance models and simulation capabilities.

The distinction between procedural knowledge and declarative (or conceptual) knowledge is not new (Cauley 1986). AI of the 1980s revealed the distinction between procedural and declarative programming. Procedural programming languages are high-level languages that allow the programmer to express an algorithm as a sequence of instructions. Some examples of procedural programming languages are

---

[6]The PRODEC methodology was developed within the FlexTech program (Boy et al. to appear).

FORTRAN (McCracken 1961; Kupferschmid 2002), Pascal (Wirth 1971), C (Prinz and Crawford 2015), and Python (Deitel and Deitel 2019). Conversely, declarative programming languages allow programmers to declare a set of objects that have properties and object-specific procedures called methods. Some examples of declarative programming languages are Prolog (Colmerauer and Roussel 1993), Haskell, Caml and SQL. These objects are then processed by a computer inference engine.

Computer science and cognitive psychology have long intersected. Indeed, the notions of procedural knowledge and declarative knowledge have been developed in several fields related to cognition, such as the educational sciences (McCormick 1997) and developmental psychology (Schneider et al. 2011), including mathematics education (Star 2005; Hiebert and Lefevre 1986; Carpenter 1986), user modeling (Corbett and Anderson 1994), experimental psychology (Willingham et al. 1989; Lewicki et al. 1987).

If we use the metaphor of theatre, a play is usually available procedurally in the first place. A writer produces an essay that tells a story. Then a director selects, in a declarative manner, the actors who are to read the essay and learn their roles and the script in a procedural manner. The PRODEC method has been designed for use in HCD in order to benefit both from operational experience (i.e., human operators will be asked to tell their main operational stories) and from the definition of the objects and agents involved in the human–machine system to be designed (i.e., the design team will progressively develop increasingly mature prototypes).

First of all, PRODEC makes it possible to explore how operations are performed before starting any development. A procedural scenario is developed with experienced people in the form of a chronology of events. The PRODEC method is based on the fact that the stories told by subject matter experts can be easily translated into procedural scenarios.

Once one or more procedural scenarios have been developed, designers are able to make explicit a set of objects and agents, which are described both functionally and structurally. These are called declarative scenarios (i.e., organizational configurations or system architecture). Of course, this articulation of procedural and declarative knowledge can, and should, be repeated as many times as necessary and possible to obtain a coherent and applicable prototype of the projected human–machine system. This prototype will be developed and validated iteratively.

The production of procedural and declarative knowledge is guided by a framework[7] that involves key factors that include the artifacts to be designed and developed, the users who will use them, the different tasks to be performed by these agents, the organizational environment where they will be deployed, and the different critical situations in which these tasks will be performed.

At this point, let's give an example of PRODEC using BPMN (Business Process Model Notation) and CFA (Cognitive Function Analysis). It should be noted that other procedural and declarative methods and tools than BPMN and CFA could be used to instantiate the PRODEC method.

---

[7]This framework is the AUTO pyramid already described in Chap. 2.

BPMN is a standard for business process modeling and a language for obtaining procedural knowledge and formalizing it graphically (White 2004; White and Bock 2011). BPMN is based on a flowcharting technique adapted to the creation of graphical models of process operations, similar to UML (Unified Modeling Language) activity diagrams. BPMN is procedural (i.e., it allows the description of procedural information with different graphical elements in the form of scripts, episodes, sequences, etc., which mixes the modes of interaction of agents with each other—it is a program or a routine in the computer sense).

The concept of a system has been defined as a representation of a human and/or machine entity. Today, machines have cognitive functions and structures, just like people. This systemic approach leads to the definition of a system as a declarative recursive entity (Fig. 2.2). CFA methodology was developed to identify cognitive (and physical) functions of humans and machines, and their interrelationships, to support HCD (Boy 1998). CFA was initially developed and used in conjunction with the iBlock representation of procedural knowledge. An iBlock, or interaction block, includes five attributes: a context of use; a set of initial conditions; an algorithm of actions; a set of normal final conditions, or goal to be reached once the iBlock is executed; and a set of abnormal final conditions. Both normal and abnormal final conditions are departures toward new iBlocks. iBlocks were used for the development of procedural interfaces (Boy 2002). BPMN provides a tool for the implementation of iBlocks.

CFA is a method for generating declarative (functional) knowledge. It has now been extended to Cognitive and Physical Structures and Functions Analysis (CPSFA).

The BPMN-CPSFA PRODEC method is then as follows:

1. Identify and review all tasks necessary to achieve the various objectives;
2. Describe them in the form of BPMN graphs (procedural scenarios);
3. Identify meaningful cognitive (and physical) functions in the form of role (associated with tasks and objectives), context and associated resources (declarative scenarios);
4. Describe and refine relevant elicited resources in terms of structures and functions (using the CPSFA formalism);
5. Iterate until a satisfactory solution is found.

Resources are generally human and/or machine agents, in the AI sense, and systems, in the systems engineering sense. Contexts express persistent situations that may be normal, abnormal or emergency. Contexts are generally defined as combined spatiotemporal conditions. For example, a postman use in a normal context may be expressed in terms of time (i.e., each day of the week from 8:00 a.m. to 5:00 p.m.), and space (i.e., a well-defined neighborhood).

The PRODEC method has been used in an air combat system project called MOHICAN (Boy et al. 2020).[8] This project aimed to derive performance measures to evaluate collaboration between pilots and cognitive systems, as well as trust in these cognitive systems. Prior to obtaining such measures, it was mandatory to

[8]The author thanks the DGA (French MOD) and Thales that supported the funding of this study and the "Man Machine Teaming" scientific program in which this research project is taking place.

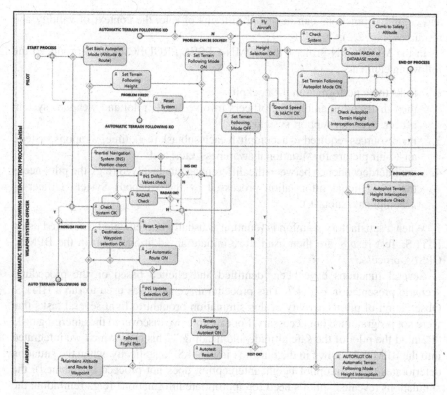

Fig. 4.7 Example of a military process for very low altitude flight without visibility, using radar (as a sensor for terrain tracking) and autopilot, involving three agents (pilot, weapons system manager and aircraft system)[9]

obtain the various human and machine functions on which these measures would be applied. First, we developed task analyses in the form of procedural scenarios (i.e., BPMN graphs). Figure 4.7 shows an example of a BPMN graph for the use case "autopilot procedure for very low altitude flights without visibility." Next, we developed function analyses in the form of declarative scenarios (agent-based configurations).

The knowledge gained on air combat functions largely determined the types of measures to be used for performance evaluation. For example, the function "Acquire Information" can be evaluated from a variety of perspectives, including accuracy, time, workload, significance, etc. The function "Acquire Information" can be evaluated from a variety of perspectives, including accuracy, time, workload, significance, etc. This depends on the context and available resources. As a reminder, physical

[9]This diagram was generated during the MOHICAN project by Julien Dezemery from Synapse Defense. Thanks Julien for your collaboration. The author thanks the DGA (French MOD) and Thales who supported the funding of this study and the "Man Machine Teaming" scientific program in which this research project was taking place.

and cognitive functions can be stated in terms of role, the context of validity and resources (Fig. 2.2).

In the MOHICAN project, the BPMN-CPSFA PRODEC process produced the following elements:

1. tasks to be performed in the cockpit;
2. their distribution among the officers involved (e.g., pilot and weapons system officer, decision support system);
3. the resources required to accomplish each subtask (e.g., time, weapons system, air-to-air picture for situational awareness, etc.) and
4. the interdependence between the different agents involved (e.g., the pilot needs the navigational information processed by the Weapons System Officer to accomplish a subtask).

When a satisfactory solution is found, it is usually implemented and tested using HITLS. Test results are then used to re-initiate an additional step in the BPMN-CPSFA process.

Several functions have been identified and elicited based on the procedural scenario presented in Fig. 4.7. This procedural scenario was used to run a HITLS. Observation of pilot's activity in this simulation brought to light several tasks that were not programmed but necessary. For example, we discovered the emerging task, "Remind the pilot of the safe altitude and heading." This task, which we integrated into the BPMN, is shown in the blue box in Fig. 4.8. Specifically, when the situation deteriorates (e.g., autopilot height interception does not proceed as planned), the simulations revealed "pilot's need for appropriate information" (e.g., reminding the pilot of the safe altitude and heading to stay on the planned route), a requirement that the experts had not anticipated in their initial procedural projections.

This example shows how emergent functions could be discovered from an initial task analysis based on procedural scenarios (left side of Fig. 4.8), which in turn are used in HITLS (middle of Fig. 4.8) with subject matter experts (e.g., pilots), leading

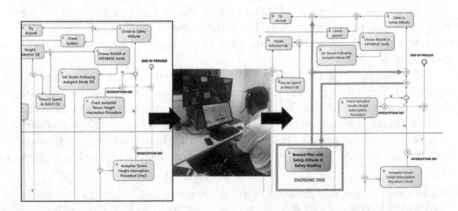

Fig. 4.8 Example of the use of PRODEC in a MOHICAN project

to the observation of activities and further analysis, and ultimately to the discovery of emergent behaviors, properties and functions (left side of Fig. 4.8).

The main emerging function involved is "collaboration," which can also be expressed in terms of role, the context of validity and resources required. We see in this example that the "collaboration" function, which implements the task of "reminding the pilot of the safe altitude and safe heading," can be assigned either to a human being (i.e., the person responsible for the weapon system) or to a machine (i.e., a virtual assistant) using an algorithm based on system status, flight parameters and minimum altitude monitoring.

PRODEC is currently used in a collaborative systems-engineering project on the development of next-generation offshore oil-and-gas facilities that involve a fleet of robots remotely managed. PRODEC provides an efficient and effective method for eliciting emerging physical and cognitive functions that have to be allocated to human operators in the operations room and the fleet of robots toward optimizing safety, efficiency, user experience, and costs.

4.6 Conclusion

HSI is a new field of investigation and practice that associates virtual human-centered design (VHCD) and systems engineering, based on virtual prototyping, human-in-the-loop simulations and tangibility metrics. Separability is a property of complex systems that enables to simplify HSI investigations. The shift from traditional engineering to digital engineering enables requirements for flexible sociotechnical systems, encapsulated in the "design for flexibility" concept. Artificial intelligence and systems engineering can cross-fertilize each other, and case-based reasoning is certainly an interesting approach to further development for HSI purposes. PRODEC is a useful method that enables a human-centered design team to elicit procedural and declarative knowledge and fulfill the gap between regular task analysis and activity analysis using virtual prototypes. PRODEC enabled to introduce the concepts of procedural and declarative scenarios. The next chapter is devoted to deepening scenario-based design, the evolution of HSI with respect to complexity and risk-taking, toward operations-centered design.

References

Bergson H (1907) L'évolution créatrice. Presses Universitaires de France, Paris. 1959, 86th edn
Boehm-Davis DA, Durso FT, Lee JD (2015) Handbook of human systems integration. American Psychological Association. ISBN-13 978–1433818288
Boy GA (2020) Human systems integration: from virtual to tangible. CRC, Taylor & Francis, Boca Raton, FL, USA
Boy GA (2021) Human systems integration and design. Chapter 2. In: Salvendy G, Kawowski W (eds) Handbook of human factors and ergonomics, 5th edn. Wiley, USA

Boy GA (2019) Cross-fertilization of human systems integration and artificial intelligence: looking for systemic flexibility. In: AI4SE: artificial intelligence for systems engineering. REUSE, Madrid, Spain

Boy GA (2016) Tangible interactive systems: grasping the real world with computers. Springer, UK. ISBN 978-3-319-30270-6

Boy GA (2013) Orchestrating human-centered design. Springer, UK

Boy GA (2002) Interfaces Procédurales [Procedural Interfaces]. National conference on human computer interaction (IHM 2002), 26–29 Nov 2002, Poitiers, France. Copyright 2002 ACM 1-58113-615-3/02/0011. ACM Digital Library (initial contribution in French, available in English upon demand)

Boy GA (1998) Cognitive function analysis. Praeger/Ablex, USA. ISBN 9781567503777

Boy GA, Dezemery J, Lu Cong Sang R, Morel C (2020). MOHICAN: human-machine performance monitoring through trust and collaboration analysis. Towards smarter design of a virtual assistant and real time optimization of machine behavior in track "Intelligent assistants, Virtual assistants, Simulation, Virtual reality". In: ICCAS symposium, ISAE-SUPAERO, Toulouse, France

Boy GA, Narkevicius J (2013) Unifying human centered design and systems engineering for human systems integration. In: Aiguier M, Boulanger F, Krob D, Marchal C (eds) Complex systems design and management. Springer, UK (2014). ISBN-13: 978-3-319-02811-8

Card SK, Moran TP, Newell A (1983) The psychology of human-computer interaction. Erlbaum, Hillsdale, NJ, USA

Carpenter TP (1986) Conceptual knowledge as a foundation for procedural knowledge. In: Hiebert J (ed) Conceptual and procedural knowledge: the case of mathematics. Lawrence Erlbaum Associates, pp 113–132

Colmerauer A, Roussel P (1993) The birth of PROLOG. ACM SIGPLAN Notices 28(3):37. https://doi.org/10.1145/155360.155362

Comte A (1998) Discours sur l'ensemble du positivisme. Flammarion, Paris, France (Originally published in 1848)

Corbett AT, Anderson JR (1994) Knowledge tracing: modeling the acquisition of procedural knowledge. User Model User-Adap Inter 4(4):253–278

Cauley KM (1986) Studying knowledge acquisition: distinctions among procedural, conceptual and logical knowledge. In: Proceedings of the 67th annual meeting of the American educational research association conference. San Francisco, CA, 16–20 Apr 1986

Deitel PJ, Deitel H (2019) Python for programmers: with big data and artificial intelligence case studies. Pearson Higher Ed. ISBN-13:978-0135224335

Gaines BR, Boose JH (1988) Knowledge acquisition for knowledge-based systems. Academic Press, Orlando, FL, USA. ISBN:0122732510

Grudin J (2009) AI and HCI: two fields divided by a common focus. AI Mag AAAI 48–57. ISSN: 0738-4602

Heidegger M (1927) Being and time. Tr. Macquarrie and Robinson (1962). Harper and Row, New York, USA

Hiebert J, Lefevre P (1986) Conceptual and procedural knowledge in mathematics: an introductory analysis. Concept Proced Knowl Case Math 2:1–27

Kolski C, Boy GA, Melançon G, Ochs M, Vanderdonckt J (2020) Cross-fertilisation between human-computer interaction and artificial intelligence. In: Marquis P, Papini O, Prade H (eds) A guided tour of artificial intelligence research. Springer Nature Switzerland AG.

Kupferschmid M (2002) Classical Fortran: programming for engineering and scientific applications. CRC Press. ISBN 978-0-8247-0802-3

Lewicki P, Czyzewska M, Hoffman H (1987) Unconscious acquisition of complex procedural knowledge. J Exp Psychol Learn Mem Cogn 13(4):523

Maturana HR, Varela FG (1980) Autopoiesis and cognition: the realization of the living. Reidel, Dordrecht

McCormick R (1997) Conceptual and procedural knowledge. Int J Technol Des Educ 7(1–2):141–159

McCracken DD (1961) A guide to FORTRAN programming. Wiley, New York. LCCN 61016618

McDermott T, DeLaurentis D, Beling P, Blackburn M, Bone M (2020) AI4SE and SE4AI: a research roadmap. InSight Special Feature. Wiley Online Library. https://doi.org/10.1002/inst.12278

Merleau-Ponty M (1964) The primacy of perception. Northwestern University Press.

Minsky M (1986) The society of mind. Touchstone book. Simon & Schuster, New York, USA

Morin E (1995) La stratégie de reliance pour l'intelligence de la complexité [The reliance strategy for complexity intelligence]. Revue Internationale de Systémique 9(2)

Norman DA (1986) Cognitive engineering. In: Norman DA, Draper SW (eds) User centered system design. Lawrence Erlbaum Associates, Hillsdale, NJ

Pavlov IP (1927) Conditional reflexes. Dover Publications, New York (1960 translation by Oxford University Press)

Pew RW (2008) Some new perspectives for introducing human systems integration into the system development process. J Cogn Eng Decis Mak 2(3):165–180

Pew RW, Mavor AS (eds) (2007) Human-system integration in the system development process: a new look. National Academy Press, Washington, DC. http://books.nap.edu/catalog/11893. Accessed May 2019

Prinz P, Crawford T (2015) C in a nutshell: the definitive reference 2nd edition. Kindle Edition. O'Reilly Media, ASIN: B0197CH96O

Rasmussen J (1983) Skills, rules, knowledge; signals, signs and symbols, and other distinctions in human performance models. IEEE Trans Syst Man Cybern 13:257–266

Schneider M, Rittle-Johnson B, Star JR (2011) Relations among conceptual knowledge, procedural knowledge, and procedural flexibility in two samples differing in prior knowledge. Dev Psychol 47(6):1525

Simon HA (1996) The sciences of the artificial, 3rd edn. The MIT Press, Cambridge, USA. ISBN-13 978-0262691918

Skinner BF (1953) Science and human behavior. Macmillan, New York, USA

Star JR (2005) Reconceptualizing procedural knowledge. J Res Math Educ 404–411

Tuomi I (1999) Corporate knowledge: theory and practice in intelligent organizations. Metaxis, Helsinki, Finland

Watson JB (1913) Psychology as the behaviorist views it. Psychol Rev 20:158–177. https://psychclassics.yorku.ca/Watson/views.htm. Accessed 25 Oct 2020

Wiener N (1948) Cybernetics: or control and communication in the animal and the machine. MIT Press, Paris, (Hermann & Cie) & Camb. Mass. ISBN 978-0-262-73009-9

Willingham DB, Nissen MJ, Bullemer P (1989) On the development of procedural knowledge. J Exp Psychol Learn Mem Cogn 15(6):1047

Winograd T (2006) Shifting viewpoints: artificial intelligence and human–computer interaction. Artif Intell 170:1256–1258. Elsevier

Wirth N (1971) The programming language Pascal. Acta Informatica 1:35–63

White SA (2004) Business process modeling notation. https://web.archive.org/web/20130818123649/http://www.omg.org/bpmn/Documents/BPMN_V1-0_May_3_2004.pdf. Accessed 23 Nov 2004

White SA, Bock C (2011) BPMN 2.0 handbook second edition: methods, concepts, case studies and standards in business process management notation. Future Strategies Inc. ISBN 978-0-9849764-0-9

Chapter 5
Activity-Based Design: Scenarios, HSI Evolution and Innovation

Abstract Scenario-based design deals with task analysis and should be complemented by human-in-the-loop simulations that enable activity observation and analysis, and therefore activity-based design. A distinction is made between task (i.e., what is prescribed) and activity (i.e., what is effectively done). The making of complex sociotechnical systems is incremental and supported by formative evaluations. HSI has evolved from human factors and ergonomics, as well as human-computer interaction. It currently merges with artificial intelligence, providing more possibilities for human-centered design. This chapter presents the evolution of engineering-oriented human-centered fields of investigation and states innovation as a risk-taking activity. Therefore, HSI results from an appropriate mix of expertise and experience from subject matter experts and creativity as a constant integration process involving technology, organization and people.

5.1 From Scenario-Based to Activity-Based Design

Scenario-based design denotes a family of techniques used in human-computer interaction (Rosson and Carroll 2002). It involves describing episodes of operations of the system to be designed through narratives. A scenario is a concrete story about use. This type of technique can only be done with the help of experts in the field in question, and at the same time, requires a great deal of creativity. It involves projecting oneself into the future and imagining plausible scenarios of operations that will be used not only to design the projected system but also to test it. This approach to scenario-based design must offer both concrete cases and flexibility in the design process. Scenarios are a tool for mediating between stakeholders, thus promoting participatory design. On the one hand, the creative guidance of scenarios offers challenges that design teams have to face and, on the other hand, the expert community of people with experience in the relevant field offers credibility in the design choices made.

One of the main challenges is to constantly evaluate the tangibility of both the digital design process and its solutions. For this, it is necessary to use tangible scenarios as well. The PRODEC method already presented above provides a

G. A. Boy, *Design for Flexibility*, Human–Computer Interaction Series,
https://doi.org/10.1007/978-3-030-76391-6_5

framework for this scenario-based design. It is first necessary to build procedural scenarios based on the experiences of field experts and professionals who are able to provide accounts of operations. Declarative knowledge about human and machine resources can be derived from these procedural descriptions.

Both types of scenarios must be realistic and cover a wide range of situations and configurations. They will serve as a basis for modeling, prototype development and subsequent testing at different levels of maturity. These tests will include human in the loop simulations using currently developed prototypes. This process is repeated until satisfactory architectural and functional results are found. This approach is commonly referred to as "agile."

Complex system design requires considering integration at three levels: technology integration, human–system integration and organizational integration. The TOP model (Fig. 3.3) supports this design approach (Boy 2013). Integration must be thought out and architected early in the design process, and not too late, as is often currently the case. Instead of designing and developing technical systems in isolation from each other, and then integrating them once they are all completed, it is preferable to have a holistic approach from the beginning, using both existing components, which could be extended or even modified during the agile design process, and/or components that are still abstract, which will be further developed for formative evaluations of the activities resulting from operations design simulations.

Scenarios need to be developed from different perspectives. First of all, the following types of scenarios should be considered: nominal (or normal) and off-nominal (i.e., abnormal and emergency). Second, the definition of the scenario should be based on past experience (e.g., successful experience as well as incidents and accidents) and on contingencies (e.g., the use of new technologies in targeted situations). Thirdly, an initial set of relevant criteria should be defined. Note that this set will be updated during agile development based on the discovery of emerging properties during testing.

Figure 5.1 presents a method based on scenarios expressed in the form of:

1. tasks and contexts;
2. roles and function/resources;
3. an evolving performance model that will serve as a reference for the iterative evaluation of the system of systems being developed;
4. activity observation and analysis;
5. using a human-in-the-loop simulation;
6. performance analysis; and
7. performance model quality testing.

This method is very related to the use of a user model at the core of Pew and Mavor's approach, as well as more recent approaches (Wallach et al. 2019; Ritter 2019). It differs by the search for performance that is based on the TOP Model (Boy 2011, 2013):

- Technology, that is, "machine agents" (e.g., usability, explainability, transparency, etc.);

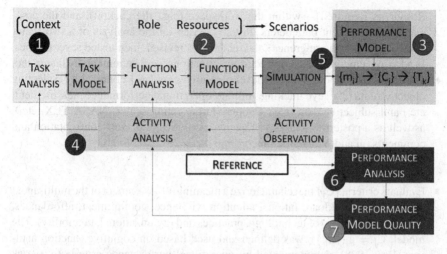

Fig. 5.1 Multi-regulated method of the formative evaluation of a human-machine system

- Organization, that is, teaming (e.g., testing trust, cooperation, coordination, cohesion, etc.);
- People, that is, "human agents" (e.g., testing workload, stress, fatigue, memory, etc.).

The human-centered design (HCD) iterative process consists of the following tasks:

- consider the main hazards of the scenario under consideration;
- identify the activities of human-machine systems that affect or interact with these hazards;
- describe the main steps of these activities, initially through task analysis and then through activity analysis (in the form of formative evaluation);
- identify the potential failures of each of the systems involved in these steps;
- identify the factors that make these failures more likely—these factors take the form of emerging functions and structures;
- use these factors to improve the system of systems by modifying its interaction logic and, if necessary, its integration logic.

In the MOHICAN project, for example, we aimed to create a solution for measuring the performance of human-machine teaming within the cockpit of a fighter aircraft. Achieving this objective required (see Fig. 5.1):

- The creation and development of a multi-agent model that represents the information and associated processing processes. We, therefore, developed a range of scenarios and contexts (i.e., the domain of use of the model), represented the cognitive and physical functions—{F} = {Role, Validity Context, Multi-Agent

Resources Required}—within the workspace (e.g., the cockpit), and the associated measurement parameters. Initially, based on the analysis of a two-seater
combat cockpit (the reference), the model was revised, then tested several times.
In addition, emerging tasks and cognitive functions were incrementally integrated.
- The model is supported by low-level measurements $\{m_i\}$ obtained by collecting
  objective data (e.g., eye tracking, military operational performance measurement,
  etc.) and subjective data (e.g., Cooper-Harper rating scales, NASA TLX, etc.),
  as well as a posteriori analysis of agents' activities (e.g., self-confrontation and
  comments on audio and video recordings).

We were able to:

- Evaluate criteria $\{C_j\}$ that characterize a meaningful assessment of the multi-agent
  system (e.g., workload, fatigue, attention, vigilance, commitment, affordances,
  flexibility, maturity [of technology, practices and organizations], tangibility). The
  model, $C_j = g_j(\{m_i\})$, was defined and used based on cognitive function analysis (Boy 1998), complemented by operational performance criteria (e.g., risk
  management, mission effectiveness, operating margin).
- Modeling teaming performance by analyzing shared situation awareness and
  human-machine cooperation, using teaming metrics $\{T_k\}$. $T_k = f_{k,context}(\{C_j\})$
  valid in a contextualized field of use.

This approach consists of implementing a method for qualifying the T_k obtained,
in order to guarantee their consistency with the operational performance observed in
the contexts studied. The MOHICAN project consists of deploying solutions (model,
method and tools) to monitor the performance of human-machine teaming that can
be reused for the definition and evaluation of future cockpits.

5.2   From HighTech to FlexTech: What Evolution?

HighTech refers to the most advanced technologies available (i.e., the most advanced
technologies available). The concept of HighTech is defined in relation to its opposite,
which is that of "simple" technology (LowTech), often mechanical as opposed to
computer technology. HighTech began to develop with electronics and integrated
circuits around the 1960s, introducing what has become modern automation.

If we focus on the uses of technologies, we can distinguish three periods (Fig. 5.2):
before the 1980s, it was the reign of mechanical technologies; the last two decades
of the 20th century saw the development of HighTech; and since the beginning of
the 21st century, we have been trying to adapt to deeply digital technologies.

Before the 1980s, Human Factors and Ergonomics (HFE) developed to fix
engineering issues, mostly on human physiological and biomechanical issues;
between the 1980s and the 2000s, Human-Computer Interaction (HCI) developed
to address cognitive issues emerging from the development of software; and since
the beginning of the 21st century, Human Systems Integration (HSI) is developing to address human-centered systemic, and more specifically sociotechnical,
issues. To summarizing, this evolution is sequentially based on a spectrum of core

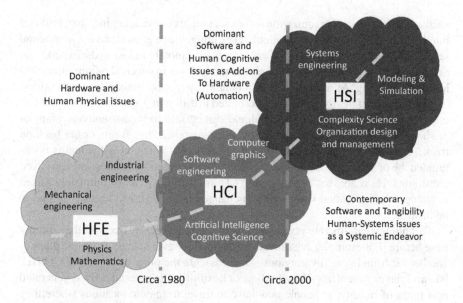

Fig. 5.2 Evolution of engineering-oriented human-centered fields of investigation

disciplines going from life sciences (e.g., medicine, physiology, neuroscience), to human sciences (e.g., clinical, experimental and cognitive psychology) and, more recently, to social sciences (i.e., sociology, anthropology and ethnography). In addition, human-centered design, which leads to human systems integration, not only includes the support of these core disciplines but also involves creativity, design thinking, complexity analysis, as well as systems engineering and science.

It must be noted that purely technological development has led to a great deal of rigidity (i.e., an obligation for human beings to adapt to machines rigidly by definition). We have gradually digitalized our societies. It is true that communication and transport technologies have opened up new possibilities, such as the availability of information at any time or the possibility of going almost anywhere very quickly. We have automated our organizational environment. We have computer tools for word processing, graphic design, calculation, collaboration and social networks that make our lives easier, at the same time as they impose rigid formats that we have to comply with.

Automation rigidifies practices because it is implemented by procedures which, by definition, are action algorithms (i.e., pre-established procedures). We have already seen that automation works perfectly when we stay within its domain of definition, but quickly diverges when we leave it. In this case, it is necessary to solve the problems we face in real time. We then need flexibility and appropriate physical and conceptual tools to ensure the success of subsequent problem solving. The epistemological bases that have enabled us to achieve HighTech must give way to new bases for the development of FlexTech (i.e., technology that support flexibility is both engineering design and operations). Notably, several scientific and technical fields are emerging, such as complexity and organization theories, complex systems engineering, artificial intelligence, modeling and simulation, 3D printing, video games, and environmental sciences. Of course, all these fields are closely or remotely linked to the exponential development of our digital societies combined with environmental requirements and human well-being. As a result, issues of tangibility are also emerging as necessities.

The concept of flexibility can be interpreted in different ways. First, being flexible requires being autonomous. An individual can be said to be autonomous when he or she is able to act without constant outside assistance "to get him or her back on track." Second, flexibility can be linked to openness. When an individual is open-minded, he or she can think and use several possible solutions without preconceived constraints. He is able to "open the box!" Third, flexibility can be intimately linked to change. An individual who is able to change his or her lifestyle easily is said to be flexible.

Technology can liberate people by giving them degrees of freedom they did not have before. For example, aviation allows people to travel quickly from one place to another far from home (by previous standards). On the other hand, before COVID, business development has taken this type of flexibility into account and has generated new types of rigidity, as people now have to travel to remote locations where they never thought they would go before, "out of obligation." Post-COVID, we may want to revise this. We often do things because they are possible, but not because they are necessary, except in an emergency. Taking care of our planet is now an emergency. Then we create new illusions of necessity. The flexibility of the possible turns into the rigidity of an artificial necessity. We must therefore be careful when we seek flexibility. For example, it is now possible to use smartphones, and many of us do so. At the same time, while this type of tool offers a lot of flexibility because we can be reached anytime and anywhere, we become mostly dependent on it, which creates an artificial necessity (for example, if for some reason we don't have our smartphone, we may miss connections or important information).

We have already discussed the transition from techno-centric engineering based on a single-agent culture to HCD based on a multi-agent culture. Let me tell you a story based on a personal driving experience in California.

This story starts with me programming a route from Berkeley to Pasadena. The car was a rental and the GPS (Global Positioning System) old and unfamiliar. I leave Berkeley in heaving traffic and follow the soothing guidance of the GPS. As my eyes dart back and forth between the dashboard and the road, I catch a short blinking message on the side of the GPS screen. It disappeared before I could read it (i.e., no significant situation was captured) and I carry on weaving my way through traffic (i.e., an attention-grabbing problem). A while later, I realized that this message might have been important, where the GPS was doing what it was meant to do (i.e., finding me an alternative route to beat the traffic). I figure this out because the route I planned from my hotel a few hours before was on Interstate 5, and I was on the 101. It is too late to turn back, and knowing this part of California well, I decide to stay on the 101. The old GPS machine was rigidly following its procedure, continuously reacting and adapting to my decisions. About two hours later (the entire trip was estimated at 6.5 h), the machine asked me to exit on the left. I did not know what to do. I continue for a while, but realize I had to make a decision at this point. I was lost. Should I trust the machine? Should I continue? I decide to trust the machine. The road becomes narrower and narrower. I have my doubts. I was ready to turn around up because the GPS didn't provide any explanation. My doubts increased when the machine asked me to go North because Pasadena was due South! I stop at a gas station and end up asking a group of people where I have to go to take Highway 5, and they all reply unanimously, "go North!," so the GPS was right!

To summarize this story, the GPS single agent was well programmed, but the mesh size of the map included in its database was very large (i.e., made of large rectangles). This property, combined with its adaptive mechanism, resulted in a two-hour longer trip (i.e., if you miss the starting point, the GPS can provide a new, much longer "optimal" route). Interviewing knowledgeable people at the gas station (i.e., a multi-agent approach) helped to increase self-confidence and trust, especially because the advice coincided with that of GPS. It is also an example of flexibility offered by competent systems.

What solutions could be brought to the problem of this GPS? The first concerns the interaction with the driver. Considering that the mapping mesh is very large, it is important to alert the driver until he has validated the reception of the information when a decision implies a certain irreversibility, in any case for a certain period of time. Another solution would be to change the mesh where possible.

5.3 Innovation Is About Risk-Taking

Specialists in human factors and ergonomics, as well as human-computer interaction, have focused for almost three decades on the development of usability engineering. It is interesting to note that what results in maximum usability of a system is standardization. Indeed, any "universal" standard communicates familiarity with the use of a system. In contrast, innovation aims to break the rigidity of traditional standards to make room for new standards. What is a standard? How is a standard established? What is the life cycle of a standard?

A standard can be established by a community of people (e.g., the International Standard Organization or ISO is an international nongovernmental organization made up of national standards bodies; it develops and publishes a wide range of standards). A standard may also emerge[1] from the success of a product (e.g., the iPhone introduced gesture-based user interfaces on mobile phones, and other manufacturers adopted this technology as a "standard"). The validity of a standard stays until a radical innovation alternative is considered and adopted by a large community of users either dictated or recognized. Innovation must therefore be seen as a breakthrough and, consequently, as risk-taking.

---

[1] This notion of emergence comes from philosophy, complexity science, systems science and the arts (Goldstein 1999; Lichtenstein 2016; Norman et al. 2018). The properties of a system qualify as emergent when they are different from the properties of its parts.

We see a trend in Western societies towards overprotection and the resulting notion of "zero risk." France, in particular, is the only country among its sister countries to have enshrined the precautionary principle[2] in its Constitution, even though this notion is officially limited to the environment. We proposed to evolve from the precautionary principle to the action principle (Boy and Brachet 2010). The French legal system has also undergone a marked evolution towards the systematic search for a culprit at the slightest suspicion that an event may have been caused, directly or indirectly, by an element of risk-taking.

We can ask ourselves why the Internet has become so popular so quickly. Concretely, the Internet is the opposite of taking risks. The Internet is an emerging phenomenon that has satisfied the needs of its users around the world. Accessibility to information has become immediate, anywhere, anytime... and all this easily. Although the U.S. Department of Defense had been developing the Arpanet network since the 1960s, the birth of the Web did not occur until 1992 thanks to the work of Tim Burnes-Lee and Robert Cailliau, computer scientists at CERN.[3] Can we talk about chance and necessity? Probably yes, because I consider creativity to be a question of integration. Internet (HTTP: HyperText Transfer Protocol) is the successful integration of hypertext and FTP (File Transfer Protocol). A lot of people have been working on these subjects for several years. I led the Computer Integrated Documentation (CID) project at NASA between 1989 and 1991, in which we not only developed an FTP-connected hypertext front end, but also installed a machine learning mechanism that added contextual elements to hypertext links based on the success or failure of interactions (Boy 1991). This type of mechanism offered more flexibility in searching for information.

Chance and necessity are not new complementary concepts; the Greek philosopher Democritus affirmed that they were the source of everything that exists in the Universe. According to Barnes, Democritus's term, chance, should be understood as an "absence of purpose" rather than as a negation of necessity (Barnes 1982). The Nobel Prize winner Jacques Monod, a pioneer of molecular biology and modern genetics, was interested in the origin of life and the evolution of species and proposed a new humanism integrating related scientific data. He argued that human beings appeared in the Universe by chance and by necessity (Monod 1970).

The management of unplanned events is one of the most crucial contemporary issues in aviation safety (Pinet and Bück 2013), and involves both chance (i.e., unforeseen events) and necessity (i.e., maintaining safety on board). Pilots are unique resources for dealing with such events and situations. For example, the recovery of the Qantas A380 around Singapore after an engine explosion on 4 November 2010 proved to be what we call a successful accident. Other successful accidents can be cited, such as the US Airways A320 that landed on the Hudson River after losing both engines on 15 January 2009; the DHL A300 aircraft that was shot down by a missile on 22 November 2003 but safely landed; and the Apollo 13 mission that

---

[2]When innovation is likely to cause harm to people when extensive scientific knowledge on the matter is lacking, we need to be cautious. We talk about the precautionary principle.

[3]*Centre d'Études et de Recherches Nucléaire* in Geneva, Switzerland.

aborted after an oxygen tank exploded on 13 April 1970. These "accidents" show that people can successfully manage very complex and vital situations when they have sufficient time and are equipped with the right functions, whether in the form of training and experience, appropriate technology, or organization; furthermore, these functions must be managed together.

This has to do with managing uncertainty. Whenever we have to make a decision in an uncertain world, we need to project ourselves into the future and anticipate what would happen if we took the appropriate actions currently planned. In other words, we either implicitly simulate possible futures in our heads, or we implement a prototype and test it using a HITLS approach, which will allow us to observe the system at work (i.e., observe the activity). Having a better sense of the activity generated in possible futures is an excellent way to manage uncertainty.

Managing the unexpected is what keeps people above systems. It is the necessary operational glue that maintains the overall stability and integrity of human-machine systems. These people must be able to understand what is happening, make their own judgments and act appropriately. Creativity is the key. These capabilities cannot be acquired without extensive training over a long period of time. Unfortunately, creativity and following procedures are contradictory concepts. That is why we need to focus more on creativity to deal with unexpected day-to-day situations instead of continuing to believe that regulations, standards and procedures are the only resources that will promote safety with this false expectation of zero risk.

Much has been said about the landing of the Airbus A320 on the Hudson River in 2009 (NTSB 2010). This successful accident demonstrated that having lost the use of all his engines over the New York City area, the captain went beyond regulatory safety rules to ensure the survival of his passengers. He decided to land on the water instead of returning to an airstrip as requested by air traffic control. Not only did this decision lead to the rescue of all passengers and crew, but it also raised the question of training pilots to follow procedures that, in some unforeseen cases, must be abandoned in favor of problem solving. From a cognitive point of view, following procedures and problem solving are different processes, involving different behaviors and skills. Following procedures presupposes that the current context corresponds to the context of the validity of the procedures used. When this is not the case, either other procedures can and in some cases must be used, or the emerging problem must be identified, posed, solved and its solution applied as a new procedure.

The current evolution of our sociotechnical environments involves contradictory issues. On the one hand, we develop more AI-based systems to enable people who are not experts to handle these systems safely, efficiently and comfortably. On the other hand, we have seen in this book that expertise and experience are key assets for handling unexpected and complex situations. Will an AI-based system make the decision to land on the Hudson River, as Captain Sullenberger, who flew his aircraft in January 2009? This system should also have glider skills. This transdisciplinary approach is becoming important, not to say crucial, today where everything is increasingly interconnected, and where it is imperative to have the ability to move from following procedures to problem-solving almost constantly. All these questions are open and should be addressed for designing technology for flexibility.

5.4 Conclusion

Flexibility cannot be obtained without enough operations knowledge. This is the reason why scenario-based design is crucial. The art of defining and developing scenarios is deeply grounded in the mastery of what this book tries to provide (see Fig. 1.1 again) associated with a confirmed practice that involves subject matter experts. HSI is the result of an evolution from HFE to HCI to complex systems design and management, and now to the massive use of digital technology toward Industry 4.0. We also should keep in mind that innovation is a matter of risk-taking that needs to be learned.

References

Barnes J (1982) The presocratic philosophers. Routledge & Kegan Paul, London

Boy GA (1991) Intelligent assistant system. Published by Academic Press, London. ISBN 0121212459

Boy GA (1998) Cognitive function analysis. Praeger/Ablex, USA. ISBN 9781567503777

Boy GA (ed) (2011) Handbook of human-machine interaction: a human-centered design approach. Ashgate, UK

Boy GA (2013) Orchestrating human-centered design. Springer, UK

Boy GA, Brachet G (2010) Risk taking: a human necessity that needs to be managed. Dossier. Air and Space Academy, France

Goldstein J (1999) Emergence as a construct: History and issues. Emergence 1(1):49–72. https://doi.org/10.1207/s15327000em0101_4

Lichtenstein B (2016) Emergence and emergents in entrepreneurship: complexity science insights into new venture creation. Entrep Res J 6(1):43–52

Monod J (1970) Le Hasard et la Nécessité: Essai sur la philosophie naturelle de la biologie moderne [Chance and necessity: an essay on the natural philosophy of modern biology]. Éditions du Seuil, coll. «Points Essais». ISBN 978-2-0812-1810-9

Norman MD, Koehler MT, Pitsko R (2018) Applied complexity science: enabling emergence through heuristics and simulations. Emergent behavior in complex systems engineering: a modeling and simulation approach, pp. 201–226

NTSB (2010) Loss of thrust in both engines after encountering a flock of birds and subsequent ditching on the Hudson River US Airways Flight 1549 Airbus A320-214, N106US Weehawken, New Jersey January 15, 2009. Accident Report NTSB/AAR-10/03 PB2010-910403. National Transportation Safety Board, Washington, D.C., USA. https://www.ntsb.gov/investigations/AccidentReports/Reports/AAR1003.pdf. Accessed 26 Oct 2020

Pinet J, Bück JC (2013) Dealing with unforeseen situations in flight—improving aviation safety. Dossier 37. Air and Space Academy. Paris, France. http://www.academie-air-espace.com/upload/doc/ressources/Doss37_eng.pdf. Accessed 12 April 2020

Ritter FE (2019) Modeling human cognitive behavior for system design. In: Scataglini S, Paul G (eds) DHM and posturography, Ch. 37. Academic Press, London, pp 517–525

Rosson MB, Carroll JM (2002) Scenario-based design. Chapter 53. In: Jacko J, Sears A (eds) The human-computer interaction handbook: fundamentals, evolving technologies and emerging applications. Lawrence Erlbaum Associates, pp. 1032–1050

Wallach DP, Fackert S, Albach V (2019) Predictive prototyping for real-world applications: a model-based evaluation approach based on the ACT-R cognitive architecture. In: DIS '19: Proceedings of the 2019 on designing interactive systems conference, pp. 1495–1502

Chapter 6
Model-Based Human Systems Integration Flexibility

Abstract Model-based human systems integration (MBHSI) extends model-based systems engineering (MBSE) by integrating virtual HCD together with the agile tangibilization of systems being developed (Boy in The handbook of model-based systems engineering. Springer, USA, 2021). This chapter presents various facets of flexibility offered by MBHSI. Complex systems deal with three kinds of issues and processes: situational awareness, embodiment and familiarity. Models can be predictive and/or knowledge based. When the complexity that they represent is put at work, it contributes to the generation of emergent behavior and properties, translated into emergent functions and structures, which are useful in agile development processes. Any sociotechnical complex system is a learning system that belongs to a class of systemic interactive models (SIM). This chapter provides an experience-driven modeling approach.

6.1 Situational Awareness, Embodiment and Familiarity

Putting us back in the multi-agent mode (system of systems), when we have to deal with a task delegation from a human agent to a high-performance and reliable machine agent, we can observe complacency (i.e., the human trusts the machine more and more blindly). Sydney Dekker has launched a debate on the circularity of complacency, intentional bias and loss of situational awareness, in which he states that complacency leads to loss of situational awareness, which in turn leads to complacency (Dekker 2015). This debate can be quickly closed if we seriously consider the distinction between awareness and consciousness (Boy 2015). Of course, consciousness includes awareness (i.e., a person's awareness of something), but it also includes being awake (Farthing 1992). In life-crtical environments, being awake implies attention and therefore not being complacent, especially when life is at stake. Complacency combines attention and critical thinking. For this reason, even if the term "awareness" will be used in this book, and in Dekker's sense, I much prefer the term "consciousness" to refer to this comprehensive concept of situational awareness that the HFE community has been using for almost over three decades.

From a complexity science point of view, consciousness can be seen as an emerging phenomenon resulting from the interaction between millions of billions of synapses and 50–100 billion neurons in the brain and the entire nervous system of a human being. No computer system can yet simulate this phenomenon. As a result, it is difficult to formally validate a digital model of consciousness to date. However, everything that is constructed by human beings (i.e., artifacts, which are also our objects of study in human-centered design) is a concrete representation of human intelligence, be it a physical object or an abstract object (i.e., cognitive or figurative). According to Jean-Pierre Changeux, the complexity of brain connectivity has increased considerably over the course of human evolution. He postulates that the Darwinian epigenetic evolution of the human brain, combined with social evolution, results in an evolution of artistic production (i.e., artistic productions are interpreted as extracerebral memories). He also argues that the human brain is not a sponge, but constantly projects, tests hypotheses, explores, organizes and engages in social communication (Changeux 2008). Consequently, consciousness must be seen as a highly non-linear dynamic process that constantly produces and refreshes our operative image, in Ochanine's sense, of the world around us, in both physical and figurative senses (Paris I Seminar on D. Ochanine's Operative Image 1981).

The complexity of the situation must be analyzed both extrinsically and intrinsically. In aviation, for example, the mental models of the pilot are progressively shaped by training and the progressive construction of experience and skills. Maturity of these mental models has a direct impact on HSI flexibility. More generally, the expertise of the human operator plays an important role when we want to analyze and evaluate situation awareness (i.e., intrinsic contribution). In addition, it is important to model operational situations, in aviation for example, to better understand the interactions between the various human and machine agents involved (i.e., the extrinsic contribution). Therefore, the expertise and experience of expert human agents (e.g., experimental test pilots in aviation) are needed to define and validate the resulting multi-agent models.

At this point, it is important to explain what we mean by complexity. First, the opposite concept of complexity is not merely simplicity, but includes familiarity. When we move from a place we know well to another part of the world, one way or another, we always find that new place complex and difficult to rationalize and manage. However, after a few months of stay, we begin to become familiar with many details coming to the fore that were previously blended in the background. We become familiar with the complex environment. Familiarity reduces the perceived complexity of the new place, for example. In other words, the emerging mental model becomes more and more familiar to the observer. Once we have learned this "familiar" mental image of the situation, it depends on how we use it (i.e., it may be located at the subconscious or conscious level of the brain, and sometimes embodied in our senses). Professional dancers, for example, have learned, through intensive training, to do jumps, spins and rotations, so they don't think at a conscious level to perform these kinds of movements. They focus on more complex activities from a tactical and strategic point of view.

Expertise and familiarity (i.e., intrinsic contribution) are not sufficient to characterize the complexity of how situations are perceived. We need to understand and deal with another type of complexity. The complexity of the available situation must also be analyzed and understood (i.e., the extrinsic contribution). A pilot cannot fly if he does not understand the physics of flight and meteorology, for example. He must have a tangible perception and understanding of the extrinsic situation of his environment. This contribution is consistent with the most commonly used definition of situation awareness in terms of perception, understanding and projection of the available situation. It should be noted that this does not eliminate the need for usability testing (Nielsen 1993) at the time of design to improve the available situation.

6.2 Predictive Versus Knowledge-Based Models

It is time to figure out what the term "model" means. Modeling is a fundamental methodological question, which can be based on two types of approaches (Fig. 6.1).

- a reactive and predictive approach based typically on an analog; or
- an intentional and experience-driven approach based on knowledge acquisition and learning.

The predictive approach is necessarily carried out in the short term. When based on mathematical equations and numerical data, prediction is necessarily constrained and limited in a given context. In this case, prediction can be expressed as a causal derivative that takes into account what has just happened in time and a model based on past experience. When a phenomenon is expressed in the form of a curve for example, the prediction of what will happened next can be expressed by the tangent to the curve (i.e., the derivative at the point of interest). We can see that we cannot go too far on the tangent; otherwise, we commit bigger and bigger errors. In addition, when this phenomenon is complex, its non-linear mathematical model is generally highly sensitive to inputs and initial conditions. However, causal prediction is not the only reactive and predictive approach. Already established mathematical models can be used, where parameters can be adapted to new contexts. Among these parameters,

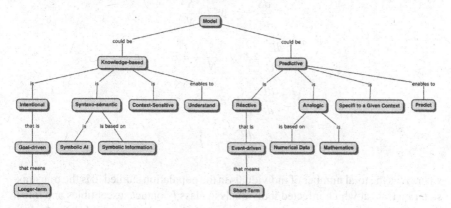

Fig. 6.1 Several types of models and their properties

initial conditions can play a crucial role, especially when models are highly non-linear, and provide misleading conclusions. An example is provided in the following paragraph.

There are several models that have been used after the COVID-19 pandemic started in Wuhan, China, in December 2019, producing a wide range of predictions. For example, in mid-March 2020, as part of the initial evolution of COVID-19, Professor Neil Ferguson, a prominent epidemiologist of Imperial College London, predicted that the UK health system could face over 500,000 deaths over the next months in England if the government took no action, and 2.2 million deaths in the United States (Adam 2020; Ferguson et al. 2020). Governments had no choice but to impose radical lockdown policies. How can such numbers be predicted using a mathematical model and initial data as sketchy as those available at the time? A follow-up question is: what is the value of these models and how should they be used? These model predictions have shown a wide range of variations due to their non-linearity nature. Roda and his colleagues (2020) showed that such wide variations were caused by non-identifiability in model calibrations using the confirmed-case data. More generally, it would be wrong to believe that modeling can predict exact numbers. This is because prediction can be believable in the very short term and, I would add, when you are lucky. The reason is that the number of parameters to be considered is so large and context-dependent that we almost always miss some of them, which may turn out to be essential in the prediction. In the COVID-19 case, prediction models were ineffective; in contrast, knowledge-based model are rather far more effective to understand the situation as a whole.

Let's take an example: the SEIR epidemiological model (Kermack & McKendrick 1927), which followed the analysis of Spanish influenza during the years 1918–1919. It is a typical knowledge-based model. It involves four equations and four variables representing four populations: susceptible (S); exposed (E); infected (I); recovered (R):

$$\frac{dS}{dt} = -\beta \cdot I \cdot \frac{S}{N}$$

$$\frac{dE}{dt} = \beta \cdot I \cdot \frac{S}{N} - \partial.E$$

$$\frac{dI}{dt} = \partial \cdot E - \gamma \cdot I$$

$$\frac{dR}{dt} = \gamma \cdot I$$

where N is the total number of individuals in the population studied, ß is the transmission rate (rate at which infected individuals in class I contact susceptibles and infect them), γ the diagnosis rate, ∂ the recovery rate (rate at which infected individuals in class I are removed from disease and become immune). The ratio $R_0 = N \cdot \beta/\gamma$, in

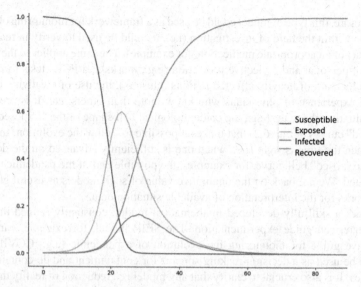

Fig. 6.2 SEIR epidemiological model[2]

its simplest form,[1] is the average number of new infections caused by an infectious individual before recovering, known as the "basic reproduction number." When R_0 > 1 the epidemic takes off and when R_0 < 1 the epidemic is negligible. Depending on the magnitude of R_0, the pandemic can develop more or less quickly. The SEIR model was used in the Fall of 2020 to simulate COVID-19 (variations of the four SEIR variables in time are presented on Fig. 6.2).

Why, in this very specific case of COVID-19, did model predictions of the evolution of the pandemic create open controversial discussions in the general public as well as the scientific community? R_0 will condition the speed and magnitude of pandemic deployment. For example, R_0 may change rapidly when people coming from another region enter into a region or when asymptomatic people carry the virus to other people without noticing it. Without sufficiently accurate and complete data, the use of such a model does not make sense because its non-linear content causes large variations of outputs to small variations of initial conditions. In fact, as sophisticated as this mathematical model is, it all depends on initial conditions and R_0 injected into it. More generally, this type of model is more descriptive (i.e., it should be used to make sense of real-world data) than predictive.

---

[1]A more complex form of R_0 can be based on the separation of several classes of infections (Mild, Severe, Critical), and include the probability that a person moves from one class to another. Therefore, a more complete mathematical description of R_0 could be:

$$R_0 = N \cdot \frac{\beta_1}{p_1 + \gamma_1} + \frac{p_1}{p_1 + \gamma_1} \cdot \left(N \cdot \frac{\beta_2}{p_2 + \gamma_2} + \frac{p_2}{p_2 + \gamma_2} \cdot N \frac{\beta_3}{\mu + \gamma_3} \right) a$$

where, p_i = rate at which infected individuals in class I_i progress to class I_{i+1}.

[2]These curves come from an academic project run by Adam Abdin and presented during the CentraleSupélec's seminar on April 30, 2020 (Abdin 2020).

Therefore, this type of model could be used as a framework for monitoring observable data within the field of investigation (i.e., it could be used to verify in real time the impact of an appropriate medication, for example). The same applies to the availability of personal and collective protection (e.g., masks and PCR[3] tests to reduce R_0), the location of heavily affected regions (clusters), the use of creativity, expertise and experience of physicians who know more than others, etc. It is precisely this qualitative character (e.g., the epidemiological bell shape of the "Exposed" and "Infected" curves in Fig. 6.2) that makes it possible to follow the evolution. In addition, when the time is right (i.e., when one is sufficiently advanced on the descent of the "Exposed" bell curve, for example), the possible end of the pandemic can be anticipated. We are back on the qualitative value of such models as useful guiding frameworks for the interpretation of available situation data.

Indeed, a skillfully developed mathematical model, constantly refined through experience, can guide experimentation. The SEIR model, for example, can be a qualitative guide for monitoring the evolution of a pandemic (e.g., COVID-19), and can be used as a decision-making support for containment and de-containment processes. It is also crucial to clarify that any model is a reduction of reality that can only be valid within its definitional context. It is, therefore, necessary to understand the genesis of a model in order to be able to use it correctly. For example, the SEIR model applied to older people (say, over 70 years of age) will not yield the same results as when applied to younger people and, as a result, may guide decision-making in very different ways. An a priori decontextualized estimation based on this type of model does not make sense.

The experience-driven approach is rooted in reality and models. This approach is based on observation of reality, expertise and knowledge, and finally making sense of real-world data—that is, understanding what is going on. A model is an abstraction of the real world it represents. It is developed and used to define observation protocols and derive predictive data (Fig. 6.3). Real-world data, obtained using observation

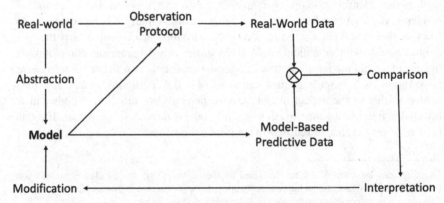

Fig. 6.3 Experience-driven modeling approach

---

[3] The Polymerase Chain Reaction (PCR) is a fast and inexpensive technique used to "amplify" small segments of DNA. Because significant amounts of a sample of DNA are necessary for molecular and genetic analyses, studies of isolated pieces of DNA are nearly impossible without PCR amplification.

protocols, are compared to model-based predictive data in order to interpret potential deviations. Derived interpretations are then used to modify the model. This iterative model-based process is repeated until satisfactory matching between real-world data and model-based predictive data is found.

In the COVID-19 pandemic case, most epidemiologists used Kermack & McKendrick's mathematical model. Such a model can obviously be used for making predictions (i.e., model-based predictive data), but without appropriate protocols for deriving real-world data, it is hazardous and even dangerous to predict anything credible.

Therefore, experience-driven models are necessary to rationalize and better understand the underlying phenomena they represent, as long as they are constantly adjusted to the real world. More specifically, based on initial assumptions, they take time to be validated. They are research models.

The experience-driven modeling approach consists of testing hypotheses and eventually validating them step by step in an agile manner, in the systems engineering sense. The underlying culture is largely based on what I already advocated, that is, observation of reality and experience. The concept of experience has two meanings: experience acquired and compiled in the form of knowledge and knowhow in a given field; and immediate proactive experience in the sense of experimentation. The experience-driven approach is empirical and requires a vision of what has to be demonstrated. It should also be noted that an experience-based model may include predictive analog models (e.g., epidemiological bell curve) when they make sense in given contexts.

Using Kermack & McKendrick's mathematical model as a guide[4] to follow the evolution of the pandemic, and more specifically, the kinetics of the number of new persons detected positive day by day (Fig. 6.4 shows such evolution for COVID-19).

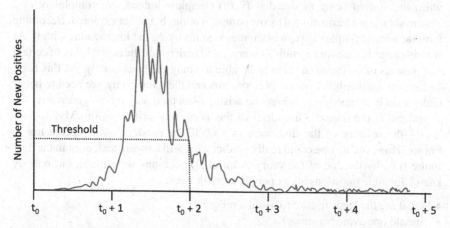

Fig. 6.4 Example of a use case displaying the number of new positive people per day from t_0 to $t_0 + 5$ months

---

[4]Complexity science showed the qualitative value of attractors. "Exposed" and "Infected" curves shapes displayed on Fig. 6.2 can be considered as attractors, which can be used as qualitative guides to follow day-by-day pandemic data. However, these shapes may vary from one pandemic variant to another. This is the difficulty when facing the unknown.

It is clear that the example of real-world data displayed in Fig. 6.4, appears noisy compared to the "Exposed" and "Infected" curves displayed in Fig. 6.2, however, the overall shape of the curve filtered of its high-frequency variability is qualitatively the same. Therefore, this qualitative aspect of the model provides an excellent guide to determine how the pandemic is progressing (i.e., the Bell curve). This experience-driven approach enables iterative (i.e., day by day) empirical identification of parameters expressed in SEIR model equations (see above).

At this point, it is crucial to clarify the type of model-based approach being used (i.e., whether the model is used to predict the future or to better understand the phenomena being studied). As a matter of fact, Fig. 6.4 can be used in both ways: for knowledge acquisition and for prediction when enough dynamics context is acquired.

We can see that using data plotted on Fig. 6.4 (built from a real-world data set) follow Kermack & McKendrick's model shape, and enable to determine the inflection point (i.e., the maximum number of new positive people), here around $t_0 + 1.5$, as well as return to negligible numbers of positive people.

This curve, when fed and used on an everyday basis, also enables the determination of when we could say that the pandemic will finish. Typically, around $t_0 + 2$, we could establish a threshold indicating that the evolution of the curvelet us anticipate that the number of positive people will be around zero in about a month. Therefore, a clear decision could be made, according to this model-based approach and acquired data in the specific context. This shows the difference between an a priori predictive approach based on a theoretical knowledge-based model and an experience-based approach that enables the accumulation of domain-specific data, useful for iterative identification of model parameters (see Fig. 6.4), which enables more credible predictions.

However, we need to be careful using the model-based approach, especially when the system being modeled is (very) complex. Indeed, the complexity of a system should not be dismissed by oversimplifications but rather explored. Becoming familiar with a complex system often means simplifying the interactions with it. As we have already seen for example, it is crucial to understand the separability of certain components of a system in order to be able to study them separately. As this book focuses on the flexibility of complex systems and their autonomy, we need to better understand how emerging phenomena arising from their activity are generated.

Indeed, at the time the first draft of this book was written—from May to July 2020—the severity of the first wave of COVID-19 pandemic was decreasing in France. However, no one could really predict what will happen next, even in the near future (i.e., by the end of the year). A lot of speculations were made, but nobody knew! Tangible questions about people's health were:

- What are the steps to take to avoid a relapse?
- Should one avoid traveling?
- How can we protect ourselves and others?
- How can we help medical staff to better anticipate and manage this multifaceted crisis, including for all of us the underlying economic crisis?
- Are there several useful models? What are the right ones to consider?
- How can they be used?

In addition, modeling does not prevent modelers from investigating the breadth of the world they want to model. In the COVID-19 case, de Weck and his colleagues (2020) proposed an extended systemic model that includes economic, financial and societal systems in addition to the purely medical pandemic model. In other words, they proposed a system-of-systems model (i.e., a multi-agent model) relevant for decision makers. Again, a major issue is the number of parameters and interconnections between these parameters, and more importantly, the presence or absence of crucial parameters due to ignorance or lack of familiarity with the complexity of the system being considered.

Last but not least, we have to admit that we are more in a logic of beliefs than a logic of truth. Why? Simply because in the model-based approach, we have an interpretation process that enables making sense of data and introduces subjectivity, and therefore a fair number of beliefs based on experience. The question is whether we should consider beliefs since the beginning as a basic foundation of complexity exploration and familiarization processes or leave it for final interpretation of data based on a logic of truth. The theory of belief revision (belief change, belief dynamics), for example, is a field of research that was born in the 1980s within the artificial intelligence community of the time. For example, Jon Doyle defined what he called truth maintenance systems (Doyle 1979). More recently, the logic of belief revision has received renewed interest (Stanford Encyclopedia of Philosophy).

6.3 Emergence and Learning Systems

A multi-agent system (i.e., a system of systems) is a living entity, which evolves according to its experience. In other words, a system learns from its experience. The complexity of a system of systems is to be identified by the interconnections between composing systems when active. For example, it is the brain activity caused by the activation of the millions of billions of links between neurons, considered as systems, that will generate an emerging phenomenon such as consciousness. Observed emergent behaviors are the result of an integration of phenomena that involve systems ranging from atomic elements (e.g., neurons) to more macroscopic structures (e.g., the brain). The emergence process is bottom-up. Emergent behaviors are the result of the implementation of emergent properties that need to be identified.

Human-in-the-loop simulations offer solid support for the observation and often the discovery of these emerging behaviors. These simulations enable testing of multiple cases in normal, abnormal and emergency situations, which often would not be possible in the real world. We will consider an emergent phenomenon as the effect of a system to be identified and need to be integrated with the system of systems being studied, such as shown in Fig. 6.5.

Emergence is a phenomenon or property that a system possesses, but not necessarily its components (i.e., its subsystems). An emergent property of a system is observed, and usually discovered, as a behavior of the system. For example, the setting in motion of a moving object emerges from the activation of a propulsion

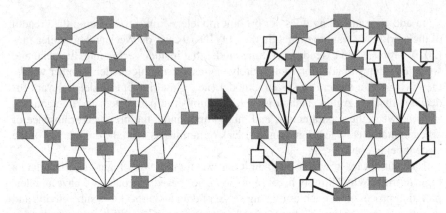

Fig. 6.5 Identification of hidden systems (white) based on observation of emergent phenomena

system that helps to overcome several resistance forces. The emergence phenomenon results from the integration of several systems that have been put into operation. For example, the life of a biological organism results from, or emerges from, the activity of several symbiotically integrated systems. Constant identification and mastery of emerging phenomena and properties, that a system has, lead to the development of its maturity (i.e., we only know that we are capable of doing something when we realize that the integration of the relevant parts of the system produces an emergent capacity). For example, you will only know that you are capable of climbing the Pic du Midi[5] when you will have actually done it, and in order to do so you will have had to correctly integrate all the human and technological capacities in the systemic sense (i.e., your physical capacities, your high-mountain skills, the necessary technical objects and so on).

At this point, we better understand why HSI requires not only task analysis, but more importantly, step-by-step activity analysis in the form of preparation (e.g., human-in-the-loop modeling and simulation), training, progressive testing and so on. Activity analysis also helps to better identify the constraints that frame the operational scope of the considered system. These constraints expressed as conditions to be met will have to be integrated into the system, thus increasing its maturity. It is also in this sense that the system is continuously learning.

6.4 Systemic Interaction Models

At this point, let's improve our understanding of how systems or agents are able to interact with each other within a system of systems (i.e., a multi-agent system). Let's consider that there are three types of organizations (Boy 2013), denoted Systemic Interaction Models (SIMs):

---

[5]The Pic du Midi is a mountain in the French Pyrenees.

Fig. 6.6 Systemic model of
supervision. Knowledge and
skills are property of the
supervisor; other agents are
performers who follow the
supervisor's instructions

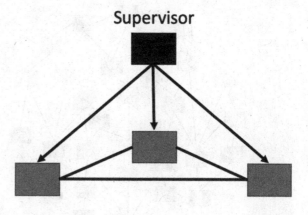

Fig. 6.7 Systemic model of
mediation

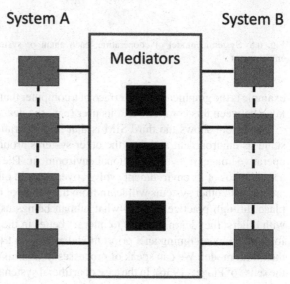

- supervision;
- mediation;
- cooperation.

Two or more agents who do not know each other (i.e., who have little or no mutual understanding of each other) require external assistance to ensure correct interactions between them. We will say that this assistance is provided by a supervisor, such as shown in Fig. 6.6.

Figure 6.7 shows the systemic model of mediation, where two populations of agents, or systems of systems A and B interact with each other using a set of mediators, in a mediation space. This is, for example, the case of two countries interacting with each other through diplomats interpreting each other's wishes. The diplomats form a mediating layer that enables for interpretations in both directions. Another

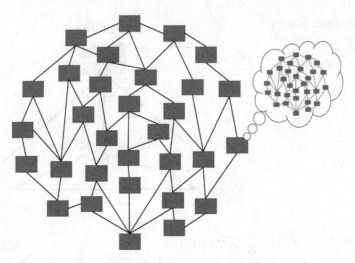

Fig. 6.8 Systemic model of cooperation: each agent or system has a "mental" model of its environment

example is the graphical user interface of a computer that constitutes such a mediating layer between this computer and its user (e.g., the desktop metaphor).

Figure 6.8 shows the third SIM is that of cooperation. Each system can understand its environment and thus the other systems around it using a socio-cognitive operative image of its organizational environment. The model of understanding that a system has of its environment evolves over time. In other words, any system cooperating with other systems will learn from the behavior of others. This learning takes place through practice. This is what human beings usually do when they interact with others; they learn in order to interact better in the future. This learning can be formalized by assigning an a priori model and/or by trial-and-error-modification of the initial model. We can speak of processes of assimilation and accommodation, in the sense of Piaget (1936). In the case of artificial systems (i.e., machines), algorithms can enable computer assimilations and accommodations to be carried out through successive functional and structural transformations and adjustments of the model for understanding the environment of a system.

The systemic model of cooperation will not only call upon questions of agent/system formalization, but also upon machine learning techniques for the construction of the internal "mental" model of each system. The notion of the mental model is borrowed here from cognitive psychology. The mental model gives an idea of what could happen if a given action were undertaken in a given context. The mental model concept is widely used in cognitive engineering and human-computer interaction (Boy 2003).

In the three SIMs, systems can be either humans or machines. For example, in the supervision SIM, the supervisor can be a human or a machine. Similarly, in the mediation SIM, mediators can be human and/or machine. A system of a

SIM, whether human or machine, will follow pre-prepared procedures when applicable in the current context or, if not, solve problems in real time (Fig. 2.1). When we talk about following procedures, we are talking about automation. When we talk about problem solving, we are talking about autonomy. Because automation is predetermined, it is necessarily rigid.

Autonomy is based on deep knowledge and experience-based skills. Sometimes a single system, human or machine, may not be able to provide complete autonomy and, in this case, it is necessary to call upon other systems to supplement the knowledge and skills required to solve the given problem. It is in this case that the systemic model of cooperation takes on its full meaning. However, it is important to note that the other two systemic models of interaction can be useful as well. For example, a "knowing" system may sometimes supervise other systems lacking specific knowledge and skills (e.g., the supervisor proposes procedures already compiled and available for abnormal and emergency situations). When a mediation service is available, it enables a set of agents to access knowledge and services more independently. FexTech is based on these SIMs that support more autonomy, coordination and flexibility.

6.5 Conclusion

HSI flexibility is a matter of maturity of underlying models. Complexity cannot usually be reduced to simple models but requires familiarity development. There are two types of models that we will consider, predictive and descriptive. It is crucial to understand their respective roles. Identification of emergent properties of a complex system is a crucial experience-based process. Human and machine systemic interaction models (supervision, mediation and cooperation) support HSI investigations and further design of increasingly autonomous, coordinated and flexible sociotechnical systems.

References

Adam D (2020) Special report: the simulations driving the world's response to COVID-19—how epidemiologists rushed to model the coronavirus pandemic. News feature. Nature (April). https://www.nature.com/articles/d41586-020-01003-6

Abdin AF (2020) Pandemic disaster preparedness model for optimal allocation of testing and hospitalization resources: the case of COVID-10. LGI seminar on safety and risk of complex systems. CentraleSupélec, Paris Saclay University, France, April 30th

Boy GA (ed) (2003) L'Ingénierie Cognitive: Interaction Homme-Machine et Cognition [The French handbook of cognitive engineering]. Hermes Sciences, Lavoisier, Paris

Boy GA (2013) Orchestrating human-centered design. Springer, UK

Boy GA (2015) On the complexity of situation awareness. Proceedings of the 19th Triennaial Congress of the International Ergonomics Association. Melbourne, Australia

Boy GA (2021) Model-based human systems integration. In: Madni AM, Augustine N (eds) The handbook of model-based systems engineering. Springer, USA

Changeux JP (2008) *Du vrai, du beau, du bien: Une nouvelle approche neuronale* [About truth, beauty and good: a new neuronal approach]. Editions Odile Jacob, Paris, France. ISBN-13: 978-2738119049

Dekker SWA (2015). The danger of losing situation awareness. Cognition, Technology and Work. https://doi.org/10.1007/s10111-015-0324-4

de Weck O, Krob D, Lefei L, Chuen Lui P, Rauzy A, Zhang X (2020) Handling the COVID-19 crisis: toward an agile model-based systems approach. Syst Eng J (Wiley, USA). http://doi.org/10.1002/sys.21557

Doyle J (1979) A truth maintenance system. Arti Intell 12:231–272

Farthing G (1992) The psychology of consciousness. Prentice Hall. ISBN 978-0-13-728668-3

Ferguson NM, Laydon D, Nedjati-Gilani G et al (2020) Impact of non-pharmaceutical interventions (NPIs) to reduce COVID-19 mortality and healthcare demand. Imperial College London (16-03-2020). https://doi.org/10.25561/77482

Kermack WO, McKendrick AG (1927) A contribution to the mathematical theory of epidemics. The Royal Society Publishing. Republished by G.T. Walker, Proc R Soc Lond A115700–721. https://doi.org/10.1098/rspa.1927.0118

Nielsen J (1993) Usability engineering. Academic Press, Boston. ISBN 0-12-518405-0

Paris I Seminar (1981) Operative image (in French). Actes d'un séminaire (1-5 juin) et recueil d'articles de D. Ochanine. Université de Paris I (Panthéon-Sorbonne), Centre d'éducation Permanente, Département d'Ergonomie et d'Écologie Humaine

Piaget J (1936) Origins of intelligence in the child. Routledge & Kegan Paul, London

Roda WC, Varughese MB, Han D, Li Y (2020) Why is it difficult to accurately predict the COVID-19 epidemic? Infect Dis Model 5:271–281

Stanford Encyclopedia of Philosophy. Logic of Belief Revision. First published Fri Apr 21, 2006; substantive revision Mon Oct 23, 2017 (retrieved on July 5, 2020: https://plato.stanford.edu/entries/logic-belief-revision)

Chapter 7
The Unavoidable Issue of Tangibility

Abstract Virtual Human-Centered Design (Virtual HCD or VHCD) is the design process using digital human-in-the-loop digital simulation. While it is now possible to explore and take into account human factors very early in the life cycle of a system (good news), the approach remains confined to a virtual environment. It is, therefore, essential to consider the tangibility of the system being developed. VHCD tangibilization process should then be considered seriously. More specifically, documenting the design process and its solution becomes essential for accessing such tangibility issues. The Design Card concept enables structuring design rationale capitalization as well as easy experience-based knowledge reuse. We then need a framework that gives us access to past experience and allows us to create solutions that address issues at hand. The evolution from MBSE to SimBSE (Simulation-Based Systems Engineering) with the human in the loop is typically supported by a multi-agent approach. Indeed, we have to consider human agents and machine agents interacting with each other. Evolutionary design versus disruptive design approaches related to the tangibility issue and metrics will be developed in this chapter.

7.1 Virtuality, Tangibility and Design Flexibility

Human-centered design (HCD) has become possible thanks to advances in digital modeling and simulation. The possibility of observing the activity and behavior of human and machine agents in a simulator from the very beginning of system design is a significant advance for HSI. We will call Virtual Human-Centered Design (Virtual HCD or VHCD) the design process using human-in-the-loop digital simulation. While it is now possible to explore and take into account human factors very early in the life cycle of a system, the approach remains confined to a virtual environment. It is therefore essential to consider the tangibility of the system being developed. Figure 7.1 shows the VHCD tangibilization process.

The term "control and management space" in Fig. 7.1 is generic, referring to a control room, cockpit, or vehicle simulator, for example. As we deliberately assume that we are in a multi-agent environment, the agents being people or machines. The first step is to place human beings, who will be involved in the control and

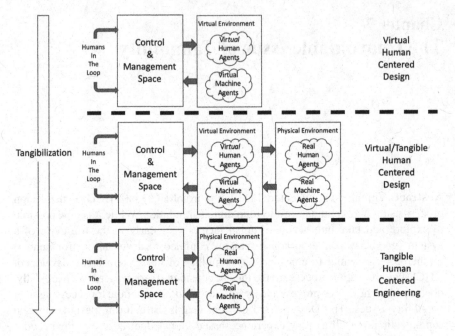

Fig. 7.1   Three-stage tangibilization process: from virtual to tangible

management of the system under design, facing a virtual system that will have to be incrementally tangibilized (i.e., gradually replace virtual subsystems by physical ones).

For example, consider that our objective is the design and development of a fleet of robots replacing people on a remote industrial platform. We will start by developing an operations room where human operators (i.e., real people) will interact with a simulator featuring a virtual fleet of robots moving and interacting with a virtual industrial platform as well. The activity of the people involved is observed and analyzed. Activity analysis results are then used to produce structural and functional modifications of the cyber-physical simulator progressively tangibilized (i.e., the playground progressively moves from the virtual to the physical). This VHCD process continues until appropriate tangibility criteria are met.

7.2   From MBSE to SimBSE with Humans in the Loop

Model-Based Systems Engineering (MBSE) is a methodology that focuses on the creation and exploitation of domain models as a mediation tool between engineers and goes beyond document-based information exchange (Long and Scott 2011).

MBSE begins with the statement of a problem to be solved (i.e., the set of system-level requirements). The problem is analyzed and translated into functional behaviors that the system must produce. These functional behaviors need to be translated into functions that need to be assigned to the most appropriate physical components (structures). The resulting system is tested to ensure that its performance meets the requirements.

One of the main problems in engineering complex systems is changing one or more of these systems once they have been prototyped, let alone when they have been developed. How can you be sure that a system is up to date? The propagation of the influences of a change on a system within a system of systems is extremely difficult, and often impossible, to track and carry out "manually." MBSE has been created and developed to take into account these changes and the propagation of their effects within a complex system. It is for this reason that a model of the system can be used to meet these needs for traceability and maintenance of changes.

Changes come from a number of causes, such as the reductionism of systemic representation, resulting in the gap to the real-world that it characterizes. A tangibility index, both physical and/or figurative, can be defined to estimate this gap (Boy 2016). Among the different attributes of tangibility, maturity should be chosen in this case. However, the stability of the systemic representation, which is expressed as its resilience to change, is also a dimensioning factor. I prefer to use the concept of stability to the concept of resilience (Hollnagel et al. 2006; Dekker and Lundström 2007; Hoffman and Hancock 2017) because it is useful to express passive and active stability (Boy 2013, 2016). In other words, the chosen systemic representation should enable modifications based on experience feedback from the real-world it models. The question here is to determine the flexibility of the systemic representation in relation to changes. In this sense, the systemic representation as a dimensioning concept of systems engineering joins that of knowledge representation in artificial intelligence. We will see in the following section how agile methods can be the driving force of the iterative process of tangibilization of a system under development (i.e., taking into account the maturity, stability and flexibility of the systemic representation at each development stage).

As introduced in the previous section, the concept of the digital twin is central to this type of approach because it allows not only to simulate behaviors of the represented system but also to link design versions of the system. The issue of managing versions of a digital twin has already been addressed by the definition of Design Cards (DC), following the earlier development of Active Design Documents (ADD) (Boy 2005, 2016).

A design card (DC) incorporates the design history of the system it represents. Multiple versions of a DC are generated and refined incrementally. These versions can be retraced at any time by any member of the design team. This traceability property of a DC has already been described (Boy 2016). It generates functionality that increases intersubjectivity within the design team (i.e., mutual understanding among design-team members).

A DC has four facets (Fig. 7.2):

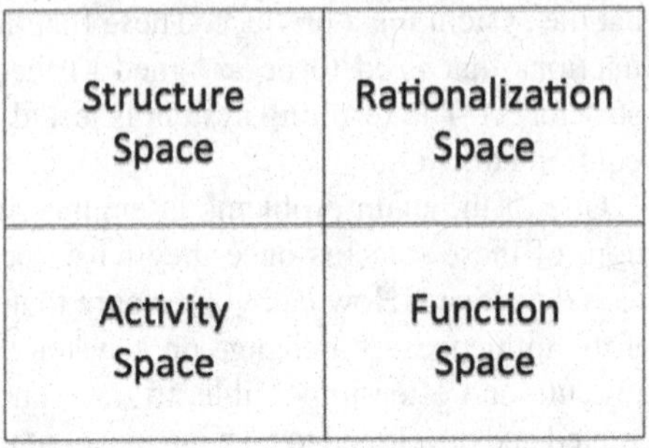

Fig. 7.2 Design card (DC)

Structure Space	Rationalization Space
Activity Space	Function Space

- A rationalization space where the various components of the system under design are described in terms of design justification, integration and requirements; this space includes descriptions in the form of declarative and procedural statements.
- An activity space where the current version of the system is available as a virtual prototype; it includes static and dynamic features; this space allows virtual HITLS (human-in-the-loop simulation) of the system.
- A space giving access to the structure of structures of the represented system where the different components and their interrelationships are described in a formal and declarative manner as systems of systems.
- A space giving access to the function of functions of the represented system where the various functions are described in terms of procedural knowledge and dynamic processes involved; this space includes qualitative and quantitative physical and cognitive models.

A given DC presents the state of a system design at a given point in time for a given design-team member (DTM). It is formally represented by the DC (t, DTM_i), where "t" is the time and DTM_i is the member "i" of the design team (note that this may be an individual or a group of individuals). A DC provides designers with a framework for describing the different components of a system of systems in the rationalization space, for displaying and manipulating them in the virtual activity space, for describing and using navigation and control functions to better conceptualize the system under development (i.e., seek more tangibility both physically and figuratively), and for filling in the evaluation space as needed after evaluating the system being designed.

The use of DCs support problem solving (e.g., removal of communication barriers related to the geographical distribution of the group's experts, improvement and/or monitoring of technological developments, staff turnover and the resolution of problems related to the lack of documentation of the design process). DCs are incrementally generated during the design process and keep being updated during the whole life cycle of a system. When DCs are documented regularly, they require very little time from the people involved. This extra time is compensated by a time saving due to a shared situation awareness by the whole design team. The quality of the DCs contributes to the quality of the design.

"What we conceive well is clearly stated..." This quote from Nicolas Boileau[1] can be taken up again in the form: "Designing is writing, and writing is designing!" In complex systems engineering, "writing" means "producing a systemic representation."

In HCD, we need to represent human or machine systems in a flexible way. DCs also support case generation, in the sense of Case-Based Reasoning (CBR), widely developed in artificial intelligence. The concept of case is commonly used in various sectors such as industry, law and medicine, for example. The case concept is often thought of as a means of categorization (i.e., generic cases). It, therefore, enables a great deal of flexibility, both cognitive and psychosocial.

Flexibility is a property that enables us to cope with changing circumstances, to think about problems and tasks in original and creative ways, and modify existing systemic patterns in a given area. This requirement for flexibility is most often necessary when unexpected events occur or when the situation becomes very complex and stressful, requiring decisions to change the state of affairs in terms of position, perspective and/or commitment. Flexibility can be considered from two perspectives:

- cognitive (i.e., the ability to process concepts fluently, sequentially and/or in parallel, in terms of mobilizing attention or reasoning resources, for example); and
- psychosocial (i.e., the ability to adapt to the demands of a situation and more generally of the environment, to balance the demands of life and to engage in behaviors).

In general, we need a framework that gives us access to past experience and allows us to create solutions that address the issues at hand. We claim that the evolution from MBSE to SimBSE (Simulation-Based Systems Engineering) with the human in the loop can only be achieved through a multi-agent approach. Indeed, we have to consider human agents and machine agents interacting with each other. Figure 7.3 shows how the SimBSE framework will support human–system integration.

We have seen that the notion of digital twin captures both modeling and simulation of the system under design and development. Among other things, it enables the design team to better understand and grasp what real, available, perceived, expected, significant (or understood), desired and projected (e.g., testing What-If) situations are. We have already discussed these types of situation and proposed a contextual model of situation awareness (Fig. 2.6).

Let's assume that we are facing a digital twin in the form of a visualization, which should be as informative as possible to provide meaningful aspects of the simulated system. For example, suppose we are performing a fault diagnosis on a complex system. The digital twin enables us to simulate the genesis of the failure in order to link and understand its causes and observed effects. Visualization of the salient parameters is therefore essential. In this case, the maintenance team must be able to "see" the system from various angles, and the identification and resolution of

---

[1]French poet and critic Nicolas Boileau-Despréaux (1636–1711), known simply as Boileau, helped reform French poetry.

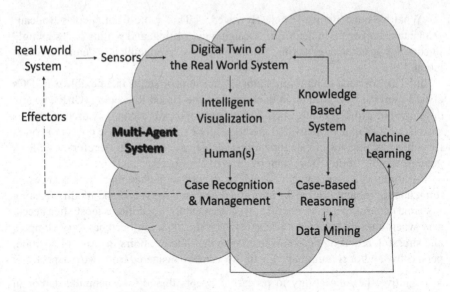

Fig. 7.3 SimBSE as an information workflow

the problem will depend, to a large extent, on the flexibility of the visualization. The digital twin will also include past experience provided by a knowledge-based system. For example, members of a maintenance team (i.e., humans) have the task of identifying known cases and giving quick answers, or similar cases and adapting solutions by analogy, or finding that the current case is new. The latter option opens the door to solving a problem that will lead to the generation of a new case that needs to be analyzed, streamlined, tested and memorized. Case-based reasoning has been the subject of much research in cognitive science and artificial intelligence (Schank 1982; Kolodner 1983; Aamodt and Plaza 1994; Begum et al. 2011). It cannot be dissociated from machine learning that underlies it.

Summarizing, SimBSE brings into play several new notions such as digital twin, intelligent visualization, case-based reasoning with the corresponding knowledge base notion, and case learning with various machine learning and data mining techniques based on experience feedback.

7.3   Planning for Systemic Flexibility

It is interesting to note that there are two communities dealing with the design of complex systems: the design engineering community (Dym and Little 2009); and the systems engineering community (INCOSE 2015). Both communities originate from industrial engineering with the following specificities: one strongly rooted in mechanical engineering; another one rooted in advanced computer science and based on a deep interest in organization theories. In other words, the first has a rather bottom-up approach and the second a top-down approach. Of course, in practice, industry always mixes the two approaches. This is why it is important to better identify the points of encounter of these two approaches to prevent pitfalls and facilitate cross-fertilization. Human–system integration is at the center of this convergence.

Design engineering is often viewed as an iterative engineering design process consisting of a series of steps that engineers use to create products. Some steps need to be repeated before the next step can begin. At each step, decisions are made based on a background in engineering science. Design engineering is implicitly single agent based (i.e., it works on the notion of quasi-isolated systems). The various phases of the process are goal and criteria setting, synthesis, analysis, construction, testing and evaluation.

Systems engineering is an interdisciplinary field of engineering sciences that focuses on designing, integrating, and managing complex systems throughout their life cycle. This notion of a system's "life cycle" and systems thinking contrasts with the design engineering approach. Systems engineering is deliberately multi-agent (i.e., a system as a system of systems), and thus opens the field of organizational issues, addressing topics such as requirements engineering, reliability, logistics, coordination of different teams, testing and evaluation, maintainability, and many other disciplines necessary for the successful design, development, implementation and ultimately decommissioning of a system that become more difficult to deal with in large or complex projects.

The Agile Manifesto (Beck et al. 2001) has been defined within the software engineering field and can be extended to other areas of engineering design. It has the following objectives:

- valuing individuals and interactions rather than processes and tools (i.e., be people-centric);
- working on software rather than complete documentation (i.e., to be product-oriented rather than process-oriented—it's the product that matters in the end!);
- working with the client in negotiating contracts (i.e., participatory design and development is essential for sociotechnical acceptability);
- responding to change according to a plan (i.e., being flexible rather than rigid throughout the life cycle of a sociotechnical system).

The AUTOS pyramid was presented based on the distinction between task (i.e., what is prescribed) and activity (i.e., what is actually done). It provides an efficient and effective framework for HCD. Therefore, designers and developers must learn and practice the art of task analysis and activity analysis. The first thing to do is to check what design and development teams are currently doing and build on this practice to establish an agile practice in the sense of the Agile Manifesto already presented. In SCRUM,[2] for example (Schwaber 1997; SCRUM 2015), it is common practice to give designers and developers a small amount of time to produce a version

---

[2]Jeff Sutherland created the SCRUM process in 1993 based on a 1986 study by Takeuchi and Nonaka (1986), Sutherland (2014), which described a new approach to increase the speed and flexibility

of the product to be designed and developed. This period is generally referred to as a "Sprint" cycle (i.e., we have represented this cycle as multiple small V's and called MVM in a previous book, Boy 2016). After performing a first cycle, it is possible to see what has been and can be done. The trick here is not to discuss what designers and developers did effectively, but how they did it. They then need to look at collaborative work and reshape the involvement of the various stakeholders to improve their production. This is what Ohno suggested for the Toyota production system long ago (Ohno 1988). In short, the only way to anticipate the duration of a project is to knowhow design and development teamwork.

When we talk about design, you we talk about creativity! What tools should we provide to facilitate creativity? Design in a given field means experience in that field! What tools should be provided to facilitate the effective incorporation of experience? These methodological and technical tools must be easy to use. They must enable a certain amount of flexibility. We have already seen that visualization and case-based reasoning techniques are good candidates to give this required flexibility. Visualization offers an essential framework that implements the advice of Napoleon Bonaparte: "A good sketch is better than a long speech!" Case-based reasoning provides conceptual support for storytelling, which is the most natural way of making expertise and experience explicit, while at the same time progressively categorizing the knowledge acquired.

De Neufville and Scholtes (2011) already presented engineering design flexibility issues and potential solutions. They focused on the creation of flexible designs they can adapt to eventualities for large-scale infrastructure systems. They addressed uncertainty of future events that may disturb the development and operations of systems. They provided technology-centered thoughts and solutions for taking advantage of new opportunities and avoid harmful losses.

7.4   Maturity of Human–System Integration

Achieving a good HSI using HCD and HITLS means that the underlying agile development process produces a tangible system at a given stage of maturity. What do we mean by maturity?

In general, we talk about Technology Readiness Levels (TRLs), but these levels are technically based only on design and development process quality. In HSI, we introduce three interconnected concepts to assess maturity:

- technological maturity (i.e., robustness, stability, controllability and observability of related technologies);
- practice maturity (i.e., related to intentionality and responsiveness of people); and
- societal maturity (i.e., culture and related organization).

---

of new product development by overlapping development phases and repeating entire development processes (multi-disciplinary, multi-functional team).

Testing maturity means discovering and rationalizing emerging behaviors, functions and sometimes structures. These emergent properties can be technological, human (or employment-related) and societal (or cultural).

Agile development is scenario-based (i.e., stories are implemented into virtual prototypes and test cases). In other words, two types of orthogonal scenarios are progressively defined and further tested using virtual prototypes and test cases (Boy et al. 2020):

- declarative scenarios that represent structural configurations (or infrastructure); and
- procedural scenarios that represent functional chronologies (or histories).

The choice of these scenarios can, of course, be very difficult. Scenario definition is currently more of an art than a technique, strongly based on experience and expertise in the field. Storytelling makes expertise and experience explicit. It is always difficult and often impossible to quantify this expertise and experience, but it is extremely useful to qualify them to guide design decision-making processes. This type of qualification is an effective way to determine the right scenarios to implement.

The shift from electromechanical cockpits to glass-cockpits in commercial aircraft motivated ergonomic studies during the 1980s and 1990s (Boy and Tessier 1985; Sarter et al. 1997). These studies focused on human factors, based on continuity of work and not on change management. Ergonomists argued that the problems were: changes in workload patterns; new demands for attention and knowledge; a break in awareness of automation patterns; new demands for coordination; need for new training approaches; new types of human error; complacency and confidence in automation. They proposed human-centered automation solutions that were not possible to implement at the time. It was not until the twenty-first century that VHCD was implemented because modeling and simulation tools and techniques have become more tangible. So, we can test systems very early during the design process.

We know today that the issue of automation surprises, which was denounced during the 1990s, is more often than not a reflection of a lack of maturity. HCD, based on formative evaluations, enables agile testing of systems under development. VHCD makes it possible to experiment and discover a large number of surprises and to correct the system accordingly, even before systems are manufactured.

In the past, automation was adapted in a progressive way by collecting feedback from the pilots who used it. It took quite some time to understand the transition from control to the management of onboard systems in aircraft cockpits. Pilots were used to controlling all critical flight parameters. A new agent, automation, suddenly took over most of those parameters. As a result, pilots had to supervise this new agent instead of controlling individual parameters, as they did in the immediate past. This change was akin to a promotion within an organization, when an employee moves from a basic job to a management position, where he or she must manage a group of people (i.e., human agents). Some of these agents do the work that a person being promoted used to do. It is sometimes tempting to micromanage when an employee is doing work that we used to do (i.e., pilots micromanaging automated systems that did the work that pilots used to do). It is essential to understand this change in practice (i.e., from control to management). This is a matter of practice maturity, which can be tested much earlier now than in the 1980s and 1990s, as HITLS capabilities and complexity analysis methods have made tremendous progress. They provide useful means to this end. Today, we can observe pilot activity using HITLS and progressively discover emerging behaviors and properties, which we could not afford to do twenty years ago. The difference is that automation is no longer an add-on, but software that is created, progressively refined and tested during the design process to meet a goal.

To summarize this discussion, automation surprises can often be related to technological maturity and/or practice maturity issues. In other words, automation should be progressively modified in a human-centered manner (i.e., adapted to user requirements), and users should be better trained to adapt to automation (i.e., users need to learn new ways to use highly automated systems). Automation design should no longer be an issue because we have the ability to develop systems holistically from the beginning in an agile manner based on human-in-the-loop simulations.

7.5   Trust, Complexity and Tangibility

Extensive research has been conducted to examine the factors that influence human trust in increasingly autonomous agents. Meta-analytic methods to existing empirical studies have been used to examine factors that influence trust (Schaefer et al. 2016). They identified three major factors of trust related to:

- machine agents based on their performance and attributes;
- human agents based on their human capabilities and characteristics; and
- the environment that includes team collaboration and task-based factors.

They found that factors related to machine agents and their performance had the greatest impact on trust. Hoff and Bashir (2015) proposed a three-level model of trust to categorize the factors that influence trust in automation:

- dispositional trust, which represents the general tendency of an individual to trust;
- situational trust, which is based on the external environment and context-dependent human characteristics; and
- acquired trust, which is knowledge of a system from past experiences or current interaction.

Learned trust is divided into two types: initially learned trust (i.e., trust before interacting with a system); and dynamic learned trust (i.e., trust formed during an interaction).

Trust is a very rich subject that has long been explored in many fields, such as psychology, sociology, human factors, philosophy, economics and political science. Trust can be intimately related to cooperation and collaboration, and thus a systemic and organizational (i.e., multi-agent) view of trust and collaboration (Castelfranchi and Falcone 2000; Mayer et al. 1995) is often required. Furthermore, and according

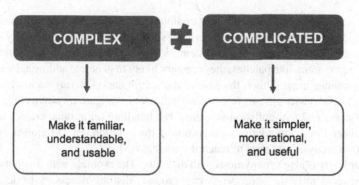

Fig. 7.4 The complex-complicated distinction

to French et al. (2018), interest in trust appears most often in situations of uncertainty and vulnerability. Furthermore, trust is needed when there is an element of risk arising from the possibility that an agent we trust may not be able to perform an allocated task (Hardin 2006).

We trust what we can grasp, physically and figuratively (conceptually). So, we trust what is tangible (i.e., what makes sense). Tangibility is a matter of complexity, maturity, stability, flexibility and sustainability (Boy 2016).

Complex does not mean complicated (Fig. 7.4). We are always looking to make a system simpler, more rational and more useful. We often create complicated products from poor design. Complex systems are complex because they have to be. The complexity comes from a necessary large number of components, interconnections between these components, feedback loops, and non-linear functions. Understanding a complex system, such as the human body, takes a great deal of time and experience.

Understanding the complexity of a system requires knowledge of that system in order to make it work. Considering familiarity seriously leads to distinguishing between several types of users, such as experts, occasional users and beginners. For example, designers and engineers who develop a system become very familiar with it and may lose the ability to explain the complexity of the system they have developed. When talking about the complex system they have developed, they may use very specific language that beginners or casual users may not understand. By analogy, musicians who speak and perform a symphony have music theory to support discussions and performances. Therefore, non-experts who observe and use a complex system should have easy and effective access to the significant parts of it in order to obtain the best possible user experience.

When system technology is mature enough, we do not worry about technology complexity. Conversely, when system technology is not mature, we need to become familiar with its complexity. For example, chauffeurs (i.e., drivers) in the early twentieth century had to know about engines and other things to perform a driving task. Today, automotive technology has become mature, and drivers do not need to know about engines and associated control systems. We need to have different knowledge (e.g., which is the nearest garage that could take my car in for repair).

Systems my become tremendously complicated because starting with simplicity in mind, designers may not consider crucial sub-systems that incrementally emerge as required from operations of the system. When they are added inside or on top of the existing system, like patches, they are very likely to generate additional workload for their management. This is the case of the accumulation of various kinds of individually useful devices in cars (e.g., speed indicators, navigation systems (e.g., GPS), vehicle status and anti-collision systems), but handling all at once creates a nightmare. Instead of accumulation, integration is the solution. HCD requires constant integration analysis and tests to reach the correct HSI.

Complexity is also synonymous with diversity. The problem with diversity is that we need to identify the appropriate backgrounds that are necessary to define and adapt the different agents not only at design time but also at operations time. In fact, the articulation of the various relevant structures and functions is crucial for humans and systems, as well as for their cognitive and physical identity. Just as we need to bring together a different set of experts to solve a complex problem, diversity requires coordination among these experts, just as musicians would need to be coordinated by a conductor to play a symphony properly.

Complexity induces difficulty. A complex system can be represented by a set of interdependent nodes. Some subsets of these nodes can be isolated and considered independently. We call this process, "separability." However, some other sets of nodes cannot be separated and must be considered together. This lack of separability leads to difficulties in analysis, design and testing. Therefore, we should always consider separability as an important process in design, especially human-centered design.

Another aspect of complexity is the contextualization of information that needs to be shared among a range of actors. This is particularly sensitive when the number of actors is large and when actors are not co-located. The question is: how can we generate a necessary and sufficient context that provides meaningful information? The context could be added in the form of verbal explanations (e.g., via a human connection between two groups), text or additional clues (e.g., visual and/or auditory). Contextualization is often linked to intentionality (i.e., it is the intention to do something that motivates the context of its realization).

7.6   Tangibility Metrics for Designing in the Virtual World

The evolution of Industry 4.0 involves digital environments that enable virtual human-centered design, which itself is based on human-in-the-loop simulations. Digital twin technology, in the form of virtual prototypes, is gradually developing. We are faced with the difficult task of defining tangibility metrics, which are inversely proportional to the distance between these digital twins and real systems they represent. This distance could be expressed in terms of confidence intervals instead of a single number (e.g., probability), where the upper limit of this interval is a possibility and the lower limit a necessity (Zadeh 1978; Dubois and Prade 2004). As a matter of fact, the probability is within this interval, and the size of the interval expresses the ignorance regarding the phenomenon.

Tangibility can be defined from two complementary perspectives: physical and figurative (Boy 2016). Physical tangibility refers to the ability of an object or system to be grasped, held and handled correctly. Figurative tangibility indicates the ability of an argument, abstraction or concept to be cognitively grasped, held or manipulated correctly. Tangibility is related to both realism and meaning. When a thing has meaning, it is tangible. It can make sense in a sensible (physical) and/or cognitive (figurative) way.

Tangibility must be assessed using appropriate properties and measures. It can be broken down into five considerations that lead to such parameters: complexity, maturity, flexibility, stability and sustainability. Some properties and measures will be provided in this chapter for illustrative purposes.

7.6.1 Complexity

We distinguish between the internal complexity and perceived complexity of a system. The former describes the parts of a system and the interconnections between these parts. When system technology is mature enough, we do not worry about internal complexity. When system technology is not mature, we need to be familiar with its complexity. This implies that human agents should be subject matter experts. When the system is technologically mature, internal complexity is no longer an issue to be considered in terms of usage.

Perceived complexity can be measured in terms of controllability (i.e., the number of controls humans need to manage the system properly) and observability (i.e., the number of sensors and indicators humans need to know how the system works). The larger these numbers, the more complex the system will be in operational terms. The consequence will be the development of more in-depth and lengthy training of human operators.

Complexity is related to the emergence of new properties. The introduction of new technologies is often motivated by a reduction in workload due to the implementation of appropriate functions and necessarily induces new roles. For example, the introduction of GPS in cars has greatly reduced driver's workload and has also induced a driving activity based on optimized navigation and consequently an overreliance on GPS. Here it is not a matter of metrics but a matter of tools and methods to identify such emergent properties.

As another example in a multi-agent system, the activity of the system can highlight the obsolescence of certain agents, and therefore their uselessness and need for replacement. The more computer assistance there is between humans and machines (i.e., virtual support), the more explicit their management (e.g., monitoring, decision and control) should be, as well as the rules of cooperation and coordination of the agents involved. This involves the emergence of new interfaces and explicit support for operations.

7.6.2   Maturity

Maturity can be analyzed and assessed using the TOP model. Technology maturity requires a better understanding of technology integration. We typically talk about technology readiness levels (TRLs). Practice maturity is related to user types, tasks and situations. Similarly, we talk about human readiness levels (HRLs). Driving a race car requires expert driving skills, knowledge and experience, which include high speed, high acceleration and acute self-preservation. Conversely, driving a family car requires a variety of skills, knowledge and experience, including moderate speed, smooth acceleration and empathy with passengers.

Organizational maturity and maturity of practice are related to various appropriate categories of agents within the organization and tasks, their interrelationships, activities produced, required skills, knowledge and experience, and organizational memory (i.e., the living experience of the organization over time). Organizational readiness levels (ORLs) should also be defined in the same way as TRLs and HRLs.

More generally, maturity is fundamentally a matter of time, of dealing with many types of events and learning. This is why human in the loop simulations and tests are essential. Different types of activities need to be tested in order to consolidate human–system integration.

7.6.3   Flexibility

Flexibility is often not a property of automation. Automation tends to rigidify activities. However, automation allows for predicting results in given contexts where automation is well defined and works perfectly. Problems arise when the context of the validity of automation is overridden at the time of operations.

Similarly, standardization (i.e., adapting people to technology) often blocks customization (i.e., adapting technology to people). Today, things change very quickly, and products must either be easily modified or replaced. Every time we start designing a new product, we have to deal with uncertainty. Reducing uncertainty leads to specific products, which involve rigid processes, but no expertise is required to use them. Dealing with uncertainty leads to open products, which imply flexibility, but require expertise.

At this point, it is essential to return on the cognitive distinction between procedure following and problem solving (go back to Fig. 1.1). When things go wrong, in a sense they are unusual and problematic, regular procedures do not work any longer. We then need to solve problems that may be new or unusual. We need flexibility, but we also need competence. In this case, we need competence in problem solving. When everything is new, it is like designing a new system. What we do in systems engineering, and more specifically in human systems integration, can be of great support. We already explained that model-based HSI (Boy 2021) could be very useful in such situations. In the COVID-19 situation, we saw that models, such as the SEIR model, could be useful conditionally to have people understanding them and knowing how to use them in an agile manner. Consequently, it would be very important in the future to have people trained in problem solving of extreme cases such as pandemics. This includes, for example, knowing about separability and complexity management of systems of systems. Again, in addition to rigid automation of technology, organizations and people (following procedures), we should head up to flexible autonomy of systems of systems, where systems include people and machines.

7.6.4 Stability

Stability can be analyzed using the TOP model. Technological stability relates to integration issues, in the sense of cyber-physical systems (i.e., how cognitive and physical components are integrated). Stability can be passive or active. Passive stability is generally related to the states of physical components that automatically (or "naturally") return to stable values when disturbed. Active stability is related to two types of agents that ensure that system states return to stable values when disturbed: (1) cognitive components (i.e., using automatic control and artificial intelligence); (2) human operators (i.e., using human skills and intelligence). Therefore, artificial or human agents have cognitive functions that need to be identified and defined more precisely. Related metrics can be domain dependent.

Organizational stability is a matter of how many reorganizations are necessary. It can be organizational evolution (i.e., involving incremental change) or revolution (i.e., involving disruptive innovation). It is often a question of the allocation of functions that requires an analysis of the cognitive functions involved. Organizational stability also concerns internal stability (i.e., the stability of the various agents/systems within the organization as a system of systems) and external stability (i.e., the stability of the organization in relation to other organizations related to it). The concept of the stability of a system of systems is crucial, as is the stability of an agency of agents (Minsky 1986). Metrics are related to trust and collaboration.

Individual (or human) stability refers to cognitive, social and emotional stability. Cognitive stability concerns internal and external cognitive support. Internal cognitive support concerns the anticipation of events, the appropriation of situational knowledge, the articulation and accumulation of knowledge, as well as risk-taking and action. Risk-taking involves experience, preparation, concentration, and proactive attitude (i.e., projecting and demonstrating a possible future). Social stability is both the individual (i.e., the stability of an individual in a group, organization or community) and collective (i.e., the stability of shared culture). Emotional stability refers to the ability to filter out disruptive signals from the environment and organization in which an individual operates. Changes in work and activities are likely to disrupt the stability of practices, depending on motivation and the difficulty in acquiring new skills and knowledge.

7.6.5   Sustainability

In engineering space system design projects such as the M2020 rover, for example, now called Perseverance, it is obvious that sustainability must be considered in terms of the longest possible life cycle once the rover is on Mars. Moreover, sustainability is a question of local autonomy and sustainable connectivity with the control center on Earth. Local autonomy should be supported by sustainable integrated systems that ensure rover's autonomy in terms of energy sources and use, information processing, communication network and mobility (e.g., wheels, legs). Local autonomy refers to the full automation local loop of the robot as a cyber-physical system. The connectivity aspect concerns technology sustainability and the type of information transferred in both directions between the rover and the control center. For the purposes of this book, information tangibility should be expressed in terms of manageable granularity (e.g., what types of task details should be sent to the robot).

It should be noted that for other systems, such as commercial components sold by suppliers, sustainability has to be expressed in different terms, mainly according to the ratio between their value and price. In this case, sustainability can be considered in two ways by asking which systems should be sustainable and which should not. Sustainable systems are generally based on value, experience and expertise. They can be costly. Conversely, disposable systems can be cheap. Some of them quickly become obsolete. In some cases, obsolescence is programmed!

7.7   Evolutionary Design Versus Disruptive Design

At this stage, we need to distinguish between evolutionary and revolutionary design. We'll talk about evolutionary design when new features are added to an existing design (for example, when a car is transformed by adding extra space or a new steering wheel). Conversely, a revolutionary design will refer to a completely new design (e.g., when a fully autonomous car—without a human driver—is built from scratch).

It may happen that the gradual modification of an existing design may lead to disruptive uses. Indeed, we need to distinguish between technology-centered evolutionary design and HCD. For example, Airbus developed fly-by-wire technology in the 1980s by progressively adding more automation to commercial aircraft. Each automated system was very useful in its own right. However, the more automated systems there were, the more difficult it was for pilots to use them all in high-pressure situations. The reason for this was that pilots were used to flying their aircraft with full control of all instruments, and most pilots did not understand that they now had to manage the new set of automated systems. This shift from control to management was disruptive from the HCD perspective, even though technology-centered engineering was seen as evolutionary. It took us some time to develop this concept ready for use! In other words, you can decide on a revolutionary or disruptive design,

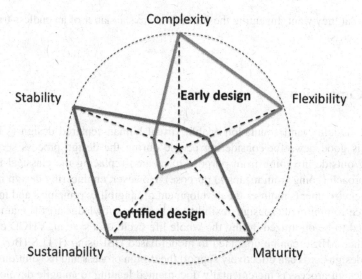

Fig. 7.5 Tangibility diagrams: (orange) first design; and certified design (green)

but you can also decide on an evolutionary technology-centered design and derive revolutionary uses from it.

We must then pay attention to the evolutionary-revolutionary distinction. We must think and act in terms of complexity, flexibility, maturity, stability and sustainability, which are the five facets of tangibility (Boy 2016). The evolution from the early stages of design to certified design (i.e., when the whole system is fully tested and validated) can be represented on five-point tangibility diagrams such as those shown in Fig. 7.5 .

Between these two extremes, there may be a range of possibilities for the five peaks. In addition, the certified-design figure shown in Fig. 7.5 is related to normal operational conditions. Under abnormal operational conditions, some of the peaks could be very different, such as the flexibility peak, which should be much higher. In addition, concepts such as maturity could be broken down into technological maturity, maturity of practice and organizational maturity, and thus lead to different patterns. Finally, these parameters have to be implemented in a large variety of cases in order to obtain emerging models and rank them.

Industry 4.0 is growing at a rapid pace based on 3D printing, digital manufacturing, lightweight materials, high-bandwidth semiconductors, composite materials, photonic integrated circuits, flexible electronics and intelligent manufacturing. Up to now, almost everything in industry is technology-driven, but very little is focused on people and organizations. I hope this book will provide some insights into the renovation of the art of design and manufacturing, where good innovation requires anticipating people's expectations and capabilities. The problem is that people's expectations can be implicit or explicit, and very often, people (i.e., users) do not know what they want. Inventing the future is always a matter of an endless trial and error process.

7.8 Conclusion

Digital modeling and simulation enable virtual human-centered design (VHCD), which is good news for considering people during the design process seriously, making outside-in (going from purpose to means) replacing the classical inside-out approach (going from means to purpose). However, engineering design in such virtual environments requires the development of tangibility principles and metrics. Resource commitments, design flexibility and system knowledge are the main issues that need to be optimized during the whole life cycle of a system. VHCD enables doing this. MBSE can be upgraded to model-based HSI using HITLS (Boy 2021) where design cards can effectively support the design process and its solutions. That is the design process is incrementally documented leading to an agile development based on the combined statement: "designing is documenting, and documenting is designing!" HSI maturity should be tested from three viewpoints: technological, practice and societal. Summing up, tangibility is a matter of trust, complexity, maturity, flexibility, stability and sustainability.

References

Aamodt A, Plaza E (1994) Case-based reasoning: foundational issues, methodological variations, and system approaches. Artif Intell Commun 7(1):39–52

Beck K et al (2001) Manifesto for Agile Software Development. Accessed 14 June 2020. http://agilemanifesto.org

Begum S, Ahmed MU, Funk P, Xiong N, Folke M (2011) Case-based reasoning systems in the health sciences: a survey of recent trends and developments. IEEE Trans Syst Man Cybern—Part C: Appl Rev. 41(4):421–434. https://doi.org/10.1109/TSMCC.2010.2071862.ISSN1094-6977

Boy GA (2021) Model-based human systems integration. In: Madni AM, Augustine N (eds) The handbook of model-based systems engineering. Springer, USA

Boy GA (2016) Tangible interactive systems: grasping the real world with computers. Springer, U.K.

Boy GA (2013) Orchestrating human-centered design. Springer, U.K.

Boy GA (2005) Knowledge management for product maturity. In: Proceedings of the international conference on knowledge capture (K-Cap'05). Banff, Canada. October. ACM Digital Library

Boy GA, Dezemery J, Hein AM, Lu Cong Sang R, Masson D, Morel C, Villeneuve E (2020) PRODEC: combining procedural and declarative knowledge for human-centered design. Technical Report. FlexTech Chair, CentraleSupélec and ESTIA, France

Boy GA, Tessier C (1985) Cockpit analysis and assessment by the message methodology. In: Proceedings of the 2nd IFAC/IFIP/IFORS/IEA conference on analysis, design and evaluation of man-machine systems, Villa-Ponti, Italy, 10–12 September. Pergamon Press, Oxford, pp 73–79

Castelfranchi C, Falcone R (2000) Trust is much more than subjective probability: mental components and sources of trust. In: Proceedings of the 33rd Hawaii international conference on system
sciences, pp 1–10. https://doi.org/10.1109/HICSS.2000.926815.

Dekker S, Lundström J (2007) From Threat and Error Management (TEM) to resilience. J Hum
Factors Aerosp Saf

de Neufville R, Scholtes S (2011) Flexibility in engineering design. MIT Press, Cambridge, USA

Dubois D, Prade H (2004) Possibilistic logic: a retrospective and prospective view 144:3–23

Dym CL, Little P (2009) Engineering design, 3rd edn. John Wiley & Sons, New York, NY

Edwards EC, Kasik DJ (1974) User experience with the CYBER graphics terminal. In: Proceedings
of VIM-21, October, pp 284–286

French B, Duenser A, Heathcote A (2018) Trust in automation—a literature review. CSIRO Report
EP184082. CSIRO, Australia

Hardin R (2006) Trust. Polity, U.K, Cambridge

Hoff K, Bashir M (2015) Trust in automation: integrating empirical evidence on factors that influence
trust. Hum Factors J Hum Factors Ergon Soc . https://doi.org/10.1177/0018720814547570

Hoffman RR, Hancock PA (2017) Measuring Resilience. Hum Factors J. 59(3):564–581. https://
doi.org/10.1177/0018720816686248

Hollnagel E, Woods DD, Leveson N (eds) (2006) Resilience engineering concepts and precepts.
Hampshire, Ashgate, U.K

INCOSE (2015) Systems engineering handbook: a guide for system life cycle processes and
activities, version 4.0. Wiley, Inc, Hoboken, NJ, USA. ISBN: 978-1-118-99940-0.

Kolodner J (1983) Reconstructive memory: a computer model. Cogn Sci 7:4

Long D, Scott Z (2011) A primer for model-based systems engineering, Vitech Corporation

Mayer RC, Davis JH, Schoorman FD (1995) An integrative model of organizational trust. Acad
Manag Rev 20:709. https://doi.org/10.2307/258792

Minsky M (1986) The society of mind. In: Touchstone book. Published by Simon & Schuster, New
York, USA

Ohno T (1988) Toyota production system: beyond large-scale production. Productivity, Cambridge,
MA, USA

Sarter NB, Woods DD, Billings CE (1997) Automation surprises. In: Salvendy G (ed) Handbook
of human factors and ergonomics. Wiley Inc., New York, USA, pp 1926–1943

Schaefer KE, Chen JY, Szalma JL, Hancock PA (2016) A meta-analysis of factors influencing the
development of trust in automation: implications for understanding autonomy in future systems.
Hum Factors 58(3):377–400

Schank R (1982) Dynamic memory: a theory of learning in computers and people. Cambridge
University Press, New York

Schwaber K (1997) Scrum development process. In: Sutherland J, Patel D, Casanave C, Miller J,
Hollowell G (eds) OOPSLA business objects design and implementation workshop proceedings.
Springer, London, U.K.

SCRUM (2015) https://www.scrum.org. Accessed 26 January 2015

Sutherland J (2014) Scrum: the art of doing twice the work in half the time. Crown Bus (September
30). ISBN-13: 978-0385346450

Takeuchi H, Nonaka I (1986) The new product development game. Harvard Bus Rev

Zadeh LA (1978) Fuzzy sets as a basis for a theory of possibility, vol 1, pp 3–28

Chapter 8
Conclusion

Abstract Summarizing, this book provides a framework for flexibility analysis in sociotechnical systems, an articulation of human systems integration (HSI) as an emerging discipline that focuses on activity-based design and innovation, model-based HSI flexibility, clarifications on sociotechnical systems, and the tangibility issue in our growing digital world. Understanding the shift from rigid automation to flexible autonomy requires a systemic framework, which is reformulated in this chapter. Digital design and engineering bring tangibility as a major issue, whereas risk taking, uncertainty management and proactive research should be primary focuses. This book presents concepts, methods and processes that support design for flexibility, but it also provides a few future challenges. Among these challenges, problem stating should be further studied and rationalized to improve problem-solving capabilities in a more flexible way.

8.1 The Need for a Systemic Framework

Design for flexibility requires a systemic framework that enables a common and consistent representation of people and machines. The notion of system can actually be considered as a representation. We talk about human systems and machine systems, which both can be described by a structure and a function that both can be physical and/or cognitive (Fig. 8.1).

This teleological definition of a system should be combined with the logical definition, which says that a system transforms a task into an activity (Fig. 2.2). Note that activity is typically observed as system's behavior. In addition, a system includes other sub-systems and often belongs to bigger systems. This induces the statement that a system is a system of systems. Consequently, a structure is also a structure of structures, and a function is a function of functions.

It follows that function allocation is a property of a system and consists of allocating a function of functions on top of a system of systems. This allocation can be deliberately done at design time, and also dynamically at operations time. Deliberate function allocation can be done incrementally after formative evaluations generating an agile development of the system. The way structures and functions are defined

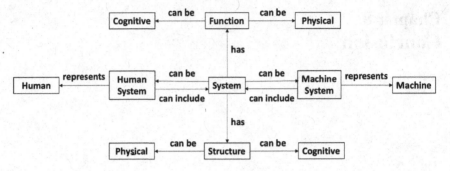

Fig. 8.1 The notion of system as a representation of people and machines

and incrementally modified strongly influence flexibility of the system in terms of system upgrade as well as activity adaptation to the context at operations time.

There are several possibilities for sociotechnical flexibility. First, systems should be intrinsically flexible in terms of structures (i.e., the architecture of a system should be designed to possibly enable easy modification of current function allocation) and functions (i.e., a function should be able to perform correctly in a wider context than initially specified). Second, systems should be extrinsically flexible in terms of possibly expended service within the systems of systems where it belongs (i.e., the service that was initially defined can be extended outside the system's context of validity). Both intrinsic flexibility and extrinsic flexibility of a system involve two crucial properties: adaptability and expendability. They both refer to services.

For example, if a machine or human service within a system can be easily replaced by an equivalent human or machine service, then the system will be said to be flexible. This kind of flexibility should exist during the whole life cycle of a (sociotechnical) system at various levels of granularity.

8.2   From Rigid Automation to Flexible Autonomy

For a long time, engineering was developed and used to overcome painful jobs and moderate the variability and roughness[1] of the world around us. The level of granularity of "systems" being used was very low compared to what we have today. Think about car maintenance! Only 60 years ago, car maintenance was very mechanical and was often done by car owners themselves. Each system was simple enough to be handled in a very simple way, when the people involved were knowledgeable, of course. Today, far fewer perform car maintenance directly. We need to go to the car dealer to maintain our car. This is because the car dealer is equipped with a digital maintenance system that enables diagnostic and repair procedures, which for most of

---

[1] The notion of roughness was introduced into the field of complex systems by Benoît Mandelbrot when he described the theory of Fractals (Mandelbrot 1983).

them are automated. When this system is mature or there is no failure, maintenance is very effective. However, when it is not fully mature or there is a failure, there is no way to return to manual maintenance—there is no flexibility. Manual reversion is at stake.

We have seen the processes of procedure following and problem solving (Fig. 1.1). Procedure following, whether managed by humans or machines (i.e., automation), has to be done within well-defined contexts of validity, and leads to rigid and even dangerous behavior outside of these contexts. In such cases, problem solving processes must be implemented, in which a high degree of flexibility is often required. Beyond flexibility in design and development, it is useful to look at what flexibility means in the other phases of a system's life cycle.[2]

More generally, if we have successfully automated in many domains, we have, at the same time, rigidified the world around us to the point where some of its non-linearities come back to us to remind us of their existence. Automation has been developed in specific contexts where it mostly works successfully. However, these contexts are not always explicitly defined and often not provided to end-users. Consequently, when end-users face unexpected system behaviors at operations time, they do not know what to do most of the time. They suddenly realize that dealing with the unexpected requires flexibility and problem-solving capabilities. What kind of tools do they have to solve such problems? This is about autonomy, which can be the autonomy of people (e.g., people being a subject matter expert and/or having appropriate support tools) and machines (e.g., machines that solve problems by themselves without external help). Actual solutions are certainly between these two autonomy solutions.

Current modeling and simulation methods and tools enable us to simulate possible futures and test various kinds of scenarios. This virtual but concrete anticipation techniques are very interesting and potentially useful for the development of human and machine autonomies, in the sense we already provided. This way, it is possible to examine potential uncertainties and study how to manage them. This is what virtual human-centered design can provide, in contrast with conventional technology-centered engineering. We are able to test various kinds of non-linearities very early on during the design process and therefore find out what are the best design requirements. These virtual tools enable a paradigm shift from twentieth century's technology-centered engineering that was going from means to purpose and usages (i.e., we develop a technology first and explore what its purpose and usages are after) to twenty-first century's human-centered design that is going from purpose and usages to means (i.e., we explore the purpose and usages of a technology in modeling and

---

[2]The concept of Maintenance, Repair & Overhaul (MRO) is commonly used today in aviation maintenance processes that are strictly regulated, mandatory and periodic, generally divided into four levels of performance: (A) monthly; (B) quarterly; (C) every 12–18 months; and (D) every 4–5 years. However, sometimes aircraft systems changes are inoperative following a flight and, in such cases, it is necessary to repair or change them without waiting for this scheduled maintenance; this is operational maintenance. Both scheduled (proactive) maintenance and operational (reactive) maintenance lead to procedure following, except in some cases that require problem solving at the last moment. In the latter cases, flexibility is required.

human-in-the-loop simulation first and find out what means should be developed and integrated later).

8.3   Digital Twins as Dynamic Documentation

Design for flexibility requires tools that increase situation awareness, decision making and action. People involved in the design of a new system should be able to easily express what should be and has been designed and developed. Up to recently, systems being designed and developed were documented using conventional documentation technology, such as text and graphics, whether on paper or electronically. As already explained in this book, modeling and simulation support design and development processes. They considerably improve design flexibility and system knowledge during the early phases of the life cycle of a system (Fig. 3.3). Modeling and simulation tools enable to develop an evolutionary digital twin of the system being design. This digital twin can be considered as a vivid representation, and therefore dynamic digital documentation, of the system being designed and developed.

Digital twins, mixing physical and cognitive modeling of real-world complex systems, enable testing "what if" possible futures and, most interestingly, potential usages and activities. These complex systems can be as diverse as industrial facilities or living organs. Digital twins evolve over time with their real twins. We can say that digital twins document their real twin counterparts. They not only document real-world systems in details from both engineering and operations points of views, but also their entire entity in the most holistic way possible. This new type of documentation enables the description of the real system, the way of making it and the way it will be used. We gave examples of such dynamic documentation systems in the form of Active Design Document (Boy 2005) and Design Cards (Fig. 7.2).

Why digital twins can help supporting design for flexibility? It is important to document physical and cognitive structures and functions of a system in order to rationalize the way it works and the way it can be used. The more this rationalization becomes mature the more we understand how the maintain it and operate it. Engineering flexibility and operations flexibility comes from this incremental rationalization. Playing with digital twins and their tangible real-world twins tends to increase the validity of this rationalization. In addition, such digital twins are also incrementally modified toward more tangible dynamic digital documentation.

A digital twin is based on an evolutionary model, whether mathematical or symbolic. Anytime you use a model, you delegate the responsibility of its output to it. This is like delegating something to do to somebody else. Delegation is first and foremost about trusting the delegated resource. Trust is often a function of both the reliability of each resource involved and the relationships between resources. For a human being, trust is an epigenetic phenomenon (i.e., trust is not innate, it is learned from interactions with the environment). Trust in an abstract system (e.g., an audible alarm may be difficult to interpret) is linked to its figurative tangibility (i.e., understanding its internal model, its operative image). Finally, trust is a matter of tangibility.

8.4 Tangibility as a Major Issue

Human-in-the-loop simulation provides good support for virtual human-centered design (i.e., exploring, finding out and assessing relevant human factors during the design process for the definition of the best system requirement possible). However, this is true within the digital environment that virtual prototypes (i.e., digital twins) provide, assuming that this environment is close enough to the real world. We know that there is a discrepancy between these virtual prototypes and the final system to be developed. How can we estimate the distance between such virtual prototypes and their real-world counterparts?

We saw in this book that the concept of tangibility could be defined from two perspectives: physical and figurative. Physical tangibility can be described as follows: "a physical object can be grasped by your hands." Figurative tangibility can be described as follows: "an abstract object or a concept can be grasped by your mind." In a digital world, both physical tangibility and figurative tangibility are not only important to perceive, comprehend and project, in the situation awareness sense, but also to appropriate and embody in a physical way. Both concepts of tangibility have become crucial because we inverted the engineering design approach (Fig. 4.2) from the twentieth century (i.e., putting software into hardware) to the twenty-first century (i.e., putting hardware around software). The former was dealing with automation usage issues; the latter deals with tangibility issues (e.g., we now develop hardware from software with 3D printing).

Why tangibility issues have become so important in design for flexibility? We saw that human-in-the-loop simulations and consequently virtual human-centered design enable fixing most human factors problems during the design process, which potentially improves both design and operations flexibility. However, this is conditionally true assuming that both physical and figurative tangibility is insured. A tangibilization process (Fig. 7.1) should be carried out to make sure that the system will be safe, efficient and comfortable in the end. The agility of this process should provide flexibility at each step during the whole life cycle.

8.5 Risk Taking, Uncertainty Management and Proactive Research

Design for flexibility requires risk taking and proactive research. Risk taking cannot succeed or lead to success without preparation (Boy and Brachet 2010). This is the reason why human systems integration is a very busy process, where the design team needs to constantly make sure that the system being designed and developed corresponds to the expected purpose and converge toward desired usages and activities.

However, even when we have taken every precaution to act in an uncertain and dangerous environment, we must always act. It should be noted that doing nothing is an action in its own right. We must always be prepared to take risks because there is no such thing as zero risk. To prepare is to acquire and conceptualize useful skills and to improve them through training. Any risky action requires discipline and flexibility. We need to train for flexibility. On one side, it is necessary to be able to follow procedures to the letter; on the other side, we need to know how to get out of a procedure in order to solve a problem autonomously. In other words, the normative procedural framework, implying a certain rigidity, must be combined with the necessary creativity, implying a certain flexibility. This approach requires high-level competence and expertise in the domain being considered—automation will never fully support incompetent human operators in dangerous domains. It is precisely this articulation that design for flexibility will seek and implement.

We always come back to questions of uncertainty, trust, collaboration, and ultimately risk-taking. These four fundamental issues have been addressed in this book. They are intimately interrelated and depend on the agent's situational awareness. A contextual model of situation awareness (Fig. 2.6) has been proposed that defines various facets of the concept of situation. Uncertainty arises when we do not have enough information about a situation that compels us to act. The more correct information and knowledge we have, the more certain we will be to act in the right way. It is then possible to automate the corresponding tasks. Conversely, the less correct information we have, the more our judgement will be based on beliefs and levels of trust. It is precisely in these cases that we need flexibility and tools to support that flexibility toward successful outcomes. These tools, both conceptual and concrete, must enable us to improve perception through various visualization techniques, comprehension through various reasoning techniques (in the sense of artificial intelligence), and projection through various mechanisms of anticipation and advice for action.

Design for flexibility should be considered in three ways: technological (i.e., offering new tools that can be adapted and provide real support for the harmonious evolution of sociotechnical systems); organizational (e.g., building and testing new collaborative models); and/or human (e.g., rethinking work and jobs, and more commonly our everyday activities). There is an urgent need to break with our current societal prejudices according to which the industrial economy we know today cannot be changed. As Edgar Morin has just said, it is time for us to change direction (Morin 2020). New models need to be built in which we do not limit ourselves to a single independent economy-centered variable but to several other variables such as well-being, environmental sustainability, trust, empathy and cooperation. Finally, not only an interdisciplinary approach is required, but we also need a radically new and highly recognized transdisciplinary community, where research scientists and practitioners will be able to produce knowledge and values. In addition, empirical approaches to design for flexibility based on data analysis and artificial intelligence should be deeply anchored together with domain experience and expertise.

8.6 Concluding Challenges

Design for flexibility is at the heart of human systems integration (HSI) and people's experience. The first requirement that human systems integrators should have to analyze, design and/or evaluate the flexibility of a sociotechnical system is knowing what this system is about. An appropriate system representation that supports the elicitation of this requirement is therefore important to have. What are its various subsystems and the relationships with other external sociotechnical systems, whether it is included in one of them or independent of them? What are the various structures of structures and functions of the sociotechnical systems at stake? How do they relate to each other? What is the right level of granularity for the analysis? Answers to these questions cannot be given without extended practice in HSI. Both expertise and creativity are at stake here (i.e., the human systems integrator should have extended knowledge and knowhow combined with creative thinking to explore possible futures).

Rich of this knowledge and knowhow based on system representation (see Figs. 2.2 and 8.1), the human systems integrator should always anticipate possible futures, using the right dose of creativity. Anticipation cannot be successfully carried out without a set of useful heuristics that can be used in a case-based manner. These heuristics are useful when regular procedures fail or are inappropriate in the current operational context. They result from systematic experience feedback integration into human systems integrator's knowledge and skills. Without long practice, such heuristics cannot be assimilated, accommodated and properly used. This is where educated common sense enters into play.

Another challenge is to better understand what complexity means in terms of response to events. We have seen that we need flexibility when things go wrong and after unexpected events. Flexibility is a matter of problem-solving skills and support that people should know about and become experience at it. For example, ocean engineering and marine sciences researchers try to better understand the complexity of a hurricane in terms of non-linear equations that lead to chaotic responses to the variation of sea temperature and other physical factors. Chaotic phenomena are impossible to predict. This is the reason why complexity science should be taught at school and universities to inform people why complex systems are sometimes unpredictable, and no matter what sophisticated approach is taken, it is often impossible to anticipate precisely the outcomes. However, complexity science tells us about qualitative aspects of these possible outcomes, in terms of attractors and catastrophes for example (Thom 1989). This may help in strategic decision-making.

We have seen the ontological necessity to have an appropriate system representation that enables various kinds of flexible solutions to problems, such as reorganization of a sociotechnical system using human-in-the-loop simulations. However, before finding appropriate solution, one should state the problem right. Problem stating requires the flexibility required for the integration of expertise and creativity, which results from a long practice and appropriate system representation, as already described. Flexibility is related to the concept of modifiability and reversibility, which are often determined during the design process of a sociotechnical system and further by integrating emergent properties during its life cycle. The challenge here is finding out the modifiability and reversibility capabilities of systems.

Artificial intelligence (AI) and data science came back strong after almost three decades of gestation. Human-centered design (HCD) for flexibility is therefore a major issue because data inputs to AI algorithms should be as relevant and appropriate as possible to avoid incorrect and dangerous outcomes. In addition to human-centered data acquisition, AI algorithm HCD is also a major issue. How flexible are processes of modifying AI algorithms in case of wrong structural design and/or wrong function allocation? How flexible is the process of data acquisition in cases of wrong raw data acquisition? Answers to these questions are crucial for managing people's trust and collaboration with their sociotechnical systemic environment, which is increasingly digital where most tasks are delegated to machine systems. Tangibility issues arise both physically (i.e., lack of embodiment erases proprioception) and figuratively (i.e., people may have increasing difficulty to understand what is going on).

In many cases, flexibility does not go without external support and, as already said, collaboration. In other words, flexibility requires physical and/or cognitive support that goes with redundancy. Therefore, flexibility cannot be thought of without a system-of-systems framework, where some systems are resources for other systems. Indeed, provision of the appropriate resource at the right time is key for success, because they can provide effective support requested for the accomplishment of a mission or a goal. Conversely, when resources are scarce, procedural support remains the only possibility, which in some cases can lead to rigidity and sometimes disastrous results. Therefore, the right number of resources is a real challenge for the proper functioning of a sociotechnical system.

The ultimate grand challenge I would like to mention is HSI flexibility in terms of sustainability, that is its contribution for society, environment and economy. At the societal level, people should be trained on flexibility issues, not only on procedure following but also on problem solving. Organizational support should also be provided for crisis management, even for light crises. Technology should be designed and developed for HSI flexibility. At the environmental level, purpose for design and development of technology should be clearly set with nature preservation goals. Organizational models should be setup to minimize transportation distances and, at the same time, enabling easy long distance transportation capabilities when catastrophic problems should be solved, for example. Motivation and cooperation among people should be facilitated and encouraged. Technology- and legal-centered solutions in terms of economy will always be a source of rigidity in specific cases resulting from the non-linearities of the complex sociotechnical systems under consideration. In contrast, human-centered solutions require democratic participatory analysis, involving stakeholders, of how human systems integration should be developed. The right mix between order and freedom will have to be constantly explored, analyzed and implemented in our sociotechnical systems, to provide good flexibility of action for all citizens.

References

Boy GA (2005) Knowledge management for product maturity. Proceedings of the International Conference on Knowledge Capture (K-Cap'05). Banff, Canada. October. ACM Digital Library

Boy GA, Brachet G (2010) Risk taking: a human necessity that needs to be managed. Dossier, Air and Space Academy, France

Mandelbrot BB (1983) The fractal geometry of nature. Macmillan. ISBN 978-0-7167-1186-5

Morin E (2020) Changeons de Voie [Let's Change the Lane]. Denoël, Paris

Thom R (1989) Structural stability and morphogenesis: an outline of a general theory of models. Addison-Wesley, Reading, MA

Glossary

Abduction Abductive reasoning is a logical inference that seeks to find the simplest and most likely conclusion from the observations based on heuristics coming from experience. In cognitive psychology, an abduction is a form of intuitive reasoning that consists in suppressing improbable solutions. This notion is opposed to a logic of systematic search exploration.

Active Design Document (ADD) Electronic document that includes the What, Why, How and How Much (evaluation) of a designed system. It is active for two reasons: the What possibly includes animations, movies or simulations; and the ADD is connected to other related ADDs for traceability and modification purposes.

Active stability When a system cannot manage to go back to a stable state by itself (i.e., passive stability), an external resource is required to keep it stable through active support.

Activity analysis Activity is the effective result of the execution of a task. Activity analysis is the process that supports the observation of activity and its interpretation.

Affordance The relationship between a human and an object or machine that enables to suggest an action by the human is called an affordance. An object or machine may have several affordances (e.g., some door handles suggest pushing, some others suggest pulling). The affordance of a system can be described as the relationship between its structure and its function (i.e., a structure suggesting a function).

Agile Manifesto Manifesto for Agile Software Development is expressed in terms of four statements: Individuals and interactions over processes and tools; Working software over comprehensive documentation; Customer collaboration over contract negotiation; Responding to change over following a plan (https://agilemanifesto.org).

Artifact May have different meanings, but in the context of human systems integration, an artifact is anything that is built by humans.

Artificial Intelligence (AI) Intelligence is demonstrated by machines, unlike the natural intelligence displayed by humans and animals. It is usually an articulated

G. A. Boy, *Design for Flexibility*, Human–Computer Interaction Series,
https://doi.org/10.1007/978-3-030-76391-6

set of methods and tools coming from computer science, engineering, philosophy, cognitive science and other scientific fields. Data science and robotics are currently the main focus of AI.

Automation Technology that - supply people with assistance in well-defined contexts. An automaton works on the basis of procedures. There are several levels of automation going from manual control to fully automated machines.

Automation surprises When an automaton performs an action that is unexpected by a user, we talk about automation surprise. Automation surprises can be reduced by human-centered design, through activity analysis as early as possible within human-in-the-loop simulation formative evaluations, and consequently increasing technological and practice maturity.

Autonomy About an agent's ability to act with respect to its own knowledge and knowhow with minimal external support. This agent can be a human or a machine.

Autopoiesis Property of a system capable of reproducing and maintaining itself. An autopoietic system maintains its identity.

AUTOS pyramid A framework that enables a design team to consider the artifact to be designed (i.e., a system), users (i.e., people involved in the overall system), tasks to be performed, organization(s) at stake, and various situations that provide a concrete meaning to the various activities being generated. In addition, the AUTOS pyramid provides the various links between these five entities, such as task and activity analyses, requirements and technological limitations, ergonomics and interaction procedures (training), emergent properties and cultural usages, social issues, job analysis, situation awareness, situated actions, usability and usefulness, cooperation and coordination issues.

Behaviorism A psychological paradigm based on observable behavior essentially conditioned either by the mechanisms of a reflex response to a given stimulus, or by the history of the individual's interactions with his or her environment.

Black Swan Theory A metaphor describing a surprise, caused by lack of knowledge, and generating interpretation of the surprise and integration of the result into long term memory.

Case-based reasoning A cognitive science and AI paradigm that provides a tractable reasoning model based on a memory made of cases already experienced, and incrementally modified to include new cases.

Catastrophe Theory A branch of bifurcation theory in mathematics that study dynamical systems, and a specific case of singularity theory in geometry.

Cognitive Engineering An application of cognitive science, psychology and anthropology to engineering design and operations of human-machine systems. Cognitive engineering focuses on cognitive work.

Cognitive Function A function that transforms a task into an activity, and is based on its role, context of validity, and resources that are required to execute the task.

Common Sense Practical sound judgement related to everyday things that leads to an appropriate action. Common sense is usually thought as "the knack for seeing things as they are and doing things as they ought to be done."

Complexity Science Focuses on complex non-linear systems and problems that are are dynamic, unpredictable and multi-dimensional, consisting of a collection of interconnected relationships and parts.

Complex Systems Systems that produce a behavior intrinsically difficult to model due to numerous interconnections and constantly emerging properties.

Computer-Aided Design (CAD) Computer support to creation, analysis and modification of a system being designed. CAD software supports design productivity, quality improvement, documentation and subsequent manufacturing.

Context Three types of context could be distinguished: verbal context in a sentence that identifies words before and after a word to provide a meaning to it; social context in an environment that identifies objects and/or agents in the environment around a system to provide a meaning to its behavior and interactions; and historical context of an event in a sequence of events.

Controllability Property of a system that defines the appropriate control variables which enable stability of the system at stake (control theory). Controllability is the dual property of observability that defines the appropriate observable variables which enable correct awareness of what the system at stake is doing.

Cybernetics A transdisciplinary approach that supports the exploration of regulatory systems. In 1949, Norbert Wiener defined cybernetics as "the scientific study of control and communication in the animal and the machine."

Cyber-Physical Systems Systems that integrate computation, networking, and physical processes. They also represent the next larger-scale generation of embedded systems, which themselves were an evolution of automatic systems (e.g., autopilot on aircraft).

Declarative Knowledge Involves knowing "that." It presents facts.

Declarative Scenario The statement of the configuration of a system is a declarative scenario.

Design Cards (DC) Describes the status of a system in terms of rationalization (why the system exists), activity (what the system produces), its structure (what is the system from a structural point of view), and function (what is the system from a functional point of view).

Digital Engineering Modeling and simulation capabilities enable a design team to create, capture and integrate data to form a model that itself enables to simulate the system being designed in a digital (virtual) world.

Educated Common Sense When common sense results from a long-enough experience on a topic together with incremental rationalization, we can talk about educated common sense.

Emergence We talk about emergence when a system shows behaviors, and therefore properties, that its components do not have.

Emergent Phenomena In a system of systems, self-organization of components that interact among each other typically results in the creation of emergent phenomena (e.g., interaction among neurons creates the emergent phenomenon of consciousness).

Engineering Design A process that consists in stating a (usually complex) problem and solving it to further develop a system. It requires flexibility. Design thinking, human-centered design and creativity are typically used in engineering design.

Experience Is related to practice, whether it is about manipulating something, interacting with somebody, or testing a system. It results in the production of knowledge and knowhow that can be further used in situations similar to the one(s) that enabled its emergence.

Experience Feedback The process that an institution uses to document experience, whether negative or positive, to increase its organizational memory, and incrementally shape its culture and organizational knowledge and knowhow.

Expertise Specialized knowledge enables its owner to work faster, more effectively and correctly in a given domain. It is learned over longer periods of time.

Figurative Tangibility Something is tangible when it is capable of being touched or grasped. In the figurative sense, a concept, an abstraction or a statement is tangible when it can be mentally grasped by somebody else (i.e., understood).

Flight Management System (FMS) A computer system that provides pilots with advanced capabilities of flight navigation. It enables programming a flight route, and automatically executing the corresponding navigation task.

Fly-by-Wire Technology (FBW) Embedded computer systems that are able to control aircraft mechanical devices. FBW mediates pilot's flight management actions and main mechanicals parts of an aircraft.

Formative Evaluations A method and a process that enables a design team to assess a system being designed and developed, as well as use evaluation results to modify the system accordingly. Formative evaluation differs from the summative evaluation that consists of producing recommendations for certification of the system.

Fractals Recursive developments of patterns. Benoît Mandelbrot provided a theory of these complex geometrical forms.

General Practitioner (GP) Also called a family doctor. He or she differs from specialized medical doctors, such as obstetricians, cardiologists or anesthesiologists.

Glass-Cockpits An aircraft cockpit equipped with electronic flight instrument displays. Traditional electromechanical instruments were replaced in the 1980s by cathode ray tubes (CRTs), which themselves were replaced by liquid-crystal displays (LCDs).

Homeostatic A self-regulating process of a system (human or machine) is homeostatic when it manages to maintain stability by adapting internal parameters for survival of the system. Failure of such a homeostatic process usually causes the death of the system.

Human-Centered Design (HCD) An approach to problem solving, commonly used in design and management frameworks that develops solutions to problems by involving the human perspective in all steps of the problem-solving process.

Human-Computer Interaction (HCI) A computer science discipline that proposes approaches, methods and tools for the design and use of computer technology. HCI mainly focuses on computer user interfaces and user experience (UX). HCI leads to interaction design.

Human Factors and Ergonomics (HFE) A discipline that involves the application of psychological and physiological principles to the engineering and design of products, processes, and systems.

Human-in-the-loop simulations (HITLS) A mandatory tool for HCD, which enables various kinds of capabilities, including human activity observation and further analysis, testing of technology maturity and maturity of practice, and ultimately human systems integration.

Human-Machine Systems (HMS) A system that includes humans and machines interacting among each other.

Human Systems Integration (HSI) We will talk about HSI for an HMS when people and machines are well integrated. Human capabilities, skills, and needs must be considered early in the design and development process as well as throughout the development lifecycle.

Industry 4.0 The ongoing automation of traditional manufacturing and industrial practices, using modern smart technology, or also the outside-in engineering design approach that goes from purposes to means by using HITLS and HCD.

Intentionality Includes, and is sometimes seen as equivalent to, what is called "mental representation." Intentionality has to do with the directedness, about-ness, or reference of mental states—the fact that you think of or about something for example.

Interaction Block (iBlock) A representation that enables design teams to describe operations procedures by considering context, triggering conditions, actions, goals (normal final conditions) and abnormal final conditions.

Interdisciplinarity A study is interdisciplinary when two or more academic disciplines are needed to carry out it. It is about creating something by thinking across boundaries.

Key Performance Indicator (KPI) A performance measurement that enables to evaluate the success of an organization or of a particular activity in which it engages.

Linear Algebra In mathematics, vector and matrices, for example, involve linear equations that fall into the field of liner algebra.

Maturity of Practice The more people become familiar enough with the use of a system, the more the maturity of practice related to the system becomes confirmed.

Multi-Agent System A computerized system composed of multiple interacting intelligent agents is called a multi-agent system, which can solve problems that are difficult or impossible for an individual agent or a monolithic system to solve.

Model-Based Systems Engineering (MBSE) A systems-engineering methodology that focuses on creating and exploiting domain models as the primary means of information exchange between engineers, rather than on document-based information exchange.

Non-Linear System In mathematics and science, a system in which the change of the output is not proportional to the change of the input. Nonlinear problems are of interest to engineers, biologists, physicists, mathematicians, and many other scientists because most systems are inherently nonlinear in nature.

Observability In control theory, a property of a system that defines the appropriate observable variables which enable correct awareness of what the system at stake is doing, also the dual property of controllability that defines the appropriate control variables which enable stability of the system at stake.

Organizational Automation In an industry where organizational automation is integrated, as a follow-up of office automation added with computer networks and could be modeled as a fully articulated system of systems mixing people and systems.

Participatory Design An approach to design attempting to actively involve all stakeholders in the design process to help ensure the result meets their needs and is usable.

Passive stability Means that no active control is needed as errors die out without requiring corrective actions.

Phenomenology A branch of philosophy founded by Edmund Husserl, based on the study of the structures of experience and consciousness. It is a way of thinking about ourselves. It focuses on phenomena, which can be described from experiences that cannot be dichotomized into pieces.

Physical Tangibility Something is tangible when it is capable of being touched or grasped. In the physical sense, an object or a machine is tangible when it can be grasped by somebody else than its designer (i.e., affordances should be right).

Positivism Philosophy assumes that the world exists and can be dichotomized into pieces that can be studied in isolation and put back together to understand the whole. The latter assumes that the world cannot be separated into pieces and should be considered as interrelated phenomena. It promotes holistic approaches.

Problem-Solving Prior to solving a problem, the problem should be correctly understood and stated. Then, creativity is at stake for projecting possible solutions, finding out their values by evaluating their outcomes.

Procedural Knowledge Refers to the knowledge of how to perform a specific skill or task. It related to methods, procedures, checklists or dolists. Procedural knowledge is also referred to as knowhow.

Procedural Scenarios A script, a chronology of actions, events and interactions, describing an articulated high-level task is a procedural scenario.

Procedure A prescription, in terms of the steps to be taken to obtain a specific result and respecting a set of rules (e.g., the procedure to plan a flight). We often talk about operations procedures or operational procedures.

Reductionism Consists in describing phenomena in terms of other simpler or more fundamental phenomena. It is also described as an intellectual and philosophical position that interprets a complex system as the sum of its parts.Reductionism. Consists in describing phenomena in terms of other simpler or more fundamental phenomena. It is also described as an intellectual and philosophical position that interprets a complex system as the sum of its parts.

Resilience The ability of a human-machine system to absorb or avoid damage without suffering complete failure and is an objective of design, maintenance and restoration for technology, organizations and people involved.

Robustness The ability of a system to cope with machine failures or human errors during operations and cope with erroneous tasks. It is the ability to tolerate perturbations that might affect the system's integrity.

Scenario-Based Design Scenarios help a design team to figure out the various interactions among agents/systems involved in the activity of a system—a system being composed of humans and machines. Scenarios are typically used in human-in-the-loop simulations. They are typically defined using the experience of subject matter experts. John Carroll said, "Scenarios are stories. They are stories about people and their activities."

SCRUM In software engineering, an agile framework for developing, delivering, and sustaining complex products. SCRUM has been used in other fields, including research, sales, marketing and, of course, systems engineering.

Self-Organization An organization that evolves without being controlled by any external agent is self-organized. Systems of systems interact among each other to insure the stability of the overall system, which is then qualified as self-organized.

SEIR Epidemiological Model Defined by Kermack and McKendrick in 1927, it involves four equations and four variables representing four populations: susceptible (S); exposed (E); infected (I); recovered (R).

Separability Refers to the property, where some systems within a system of systems could be separated from the rest of the overall system without harming it and enabling these (sub)systems to be studied independently.

Situation Refers to a set of circumstances in which one finds oneself (e.g., a state of affairs), a location, an event, a state vector, etc., in this book, a situation can be normal, abnormal or emergency.

Situation Awareness According to Endsley's model, a sequence of three high-level cognitive functions: perception, comprehension and projection.

Socio-Cognition Specifically used when complex cognitive and social properties are reciprocally connected and essential for a given problem. Socio-cognition can be though as integration of cognitive interactions and functions into the design of a complex sociotechnical system. Various kinds of organizations can be found and studied, such as teams, communities and large institutions.

Societal Maturity A society or an organization that is mature for adopting a technology or product is said societally mature.

Sociotechnical Flexibility When agents or systems of an organization or a sociotechnical system are able to adapt easily, we will talk about sociotechnical flexibility.

Sociotechnical Maturity A combination of the three types of maturity: technological maturity; maturity of practice; and societal maturity.

Sociotechnical System Organization design and management require the definition of what a sociotechnical system is. A sociotechnical system includes people and machines working together.

Stability Adapting the concept of stability in physics, stability refers to the ability of a system to restore to its original functioning, after it has been slightly disturbed or attacked. System's stability can be either passive (i.e., original functioning is restored automatically) or active (i.e., an external assistance is necessary to restore original functioning). The concept of stability is intimately related to the concept of resilience.

Subconscious Part of the mind that is not currently in focal awareness.

Systemic Interaction Models (SIMs) There are three types of organizations useful for HSI, denoted Systemic Interaction Models: supervision; mediation; and cooperation.

Systems Engineering A transdisciplinary and integrative approach that enables the successful realization, use, and retirement of engineered systems, using systems principles and concepts, and scientific, technological, and management methods.

System of Systems (SoS) A collection of independent systems, integrated into a larger system. Constituent systems collaborate to produce global behavior that they cannot produce alone.

Tangibility Metrics There are five main attributes of tangibility: complexity, flexibility; maturity, stability and sustainability. Each of these attributes has its own metrics. Therefore, tangibility metrics result from the aggregation of several relevant attributes metrics.

Tangible Interactive Systems (TIS) Go far beyond the concept of tangible user interfaces, addressing large complex systems in the framework of human-centered design and putting the human at the center of the design process from the start and along the whole life cycle of a system.

Task Analysis The process of breaking a goal, story or procedure down into smaller, more manageable components and documenting these pieces.

Technological Maturity A technology becomes mature when flaws that prevent users from getting the full benefit of the technology are inexistant or rare. In some contexts, a technology is mature when it has been in widespread used.

Technology-Centered Engineering For a long time, technology has been designed and developed from inside-out (i.e., the kernel of the technology is developed first and people who will use it will be considered later, reinforcing the concept of user interface for hiding some clumsy part at operations time). Inside-out means that technology is designed and developed from means to purpose. Instead, human-centered design works from outside-in, that is from purpose to means.

Technology Readiness Levels (TRLs) Developed by NASA in 1970s to provide a scale for estimating technological maturity during the acquisition phase of a program. TRLs currently provide a framework for consistent, uniform discussions of technical maturity across different types of technology.

Technological Maturity The less a system is technologically mature, the more expertise on the side of people is mandatory. The more a system is technologically mature, the less expertise on the side of people is mandatory.

TOP Model (Technology—Organizations—People) A frame of reference for a design team that associates technology being developed to people who will use it and the organization in which they both will interact.

Unified Modeling Language (UML) In software engineering, a modeling language that enables the visualization of the design of a system.

Usability Engineering The process of testing the capacity of a system to provide a condition for its users to perform tasks safely, effectively, efficiently and comfortably while enjoying their experience. The term user experience or UX is commonly used for referring the current evolution of this approach.

Virtual Assistant (VA) An agent or system (human and/or machine) able to provide assistance to another agent or system, usually a computer system (e.g., a VA in an aircraft cockpit).

Virtual Human-Centered Design (VHCD) Uses virtual prototypes to enable human-in-the-loop simulations and therefore activity observation and analysis for the sake of formative evaluations and incremental HCD. VHCD should be combined with tangibility testing and incremental tangibilization.

Virtual Prototyping A method in HSI that involves using computer-aided design, automation and computer-aided engineering software to observe, analyze and validate human-in-the-loop activity and a virtual prototype before committing to making a physical prototype.

Vitalism Developed by Henri Bergson, mainly related to the reptilian brain, including emotions, experience and skills. It is also related to Nietzsche's "will to power" concept that was close to Schopenhauer's "will to live," a psychological force consciously and unconsciously used to survive.

Printed in the United States
by Baker & Taylor Publisher Services